The Myth of Population Control

The Myth of Population Control

Family, Caste, and Class
in an Indian Village

Mahmood Mamdani

Monthly Review Press
New York

Monthly Review Press
122 West 27th Street
New York, N.Y. 10001

15   14   13

Contents

To Ammy, Daddy, Anis, and Masuma

Westerners have strong feelings about the value of persons and of human life not necessarily shared by Punjabi villagers. Some readers may feel that the pressures arising from growing numbers of people were self-evident. The villagers did not always hold that view.
—John Wyon and John Gordon, directors of the Khanna Study

These Americans are enemies of the smile on this child's face. All they are interested in is war or family planning.
—A Khanna Study villager

Acknowledgments

This work began as part of a study on "Technology and Society" undertaken by a seminar at Harvard University. To my colleagues in that seminar—Michael, Margot, Carol, John, and Harvey—I am most grateful for their repeated readings and fearless criticism of the innumerable drafts that resulted in the final manuscript. During the entire period, from designing the research project to writing the essay, I received valuable guidance and continued encouragement from Professor David Landes of the Department of History and Professor Arthur MacEwan of the Department of Economics. For their assistance, which was certainly beyond the call of duty, I express my deepest thanks.

In Manupur, my learning was greatly enhanced by repeated discussions with Malkiet Singh, Shaktiprasadji, Bhajan Singh, Hakim Dilipchand, Rajkumar, and Pandit Pritamdas. They were mentors who also became good friends. The reader will have an opportunity to meet many of them in the course of these pages.

To my hosts who introduced me to various aspects of

Indian village and city life and were patient as I learned —to Malkiet Singh of Manupur, Manmohan Singh in Khanna, and to Dr. and Mrs. Sahni, to Pradeep and Titli in Delhi—I am indeed grateful. There are many who have helped me with valuable advice and assistance at one time or another: among them I must mention Professor David Heer of the Center for Population Studies at Harvard, Professor Frank Hutchins of the Department of Government, and friends Ivory Robinson and Bob Miester.

The finances for my stay in India were generously provided by the Technology and Society Program at Harvard University. Access to the documents of the Khanna Study was given me by its director, Dr. John Wyon. To both, I am most grateful.

For having made this book a little more readable and a little more sensible, my deepest thanks to Susan Lowes, who carefully and patiently edited the final version of the manuscript. After such generous assistance, if errors still remain within these pages, only I am to be blamed.

—M. M.

Introduction

Much has been written about the "population problem" in recent years. "Overpopulation" is said to be the major reason for the poverty of the "underdeveloped" countries; overpopulation is the "malaise" and family planning the "remedy." Such thinking has been popularized by various neo-Malthusian writings, including Paul Ehrlich's best selling *Population Bomb*. Ehrlich describes how the significance of the "population problem" dawned on him suddenly "one stinking hot night in Delhi":

> As we crawled through the city [in a taxi], we entered a crowded slum area. The temperature was well over 100, and the air was a haze of dust and smoke. The streets seemed alive with people. People eating, people washing, people sleeping. People visiting, arguing and screaming. People thrusting their hands through the taxi window, begging. People defecating and urinating. People clinging to buses. People herding animals. People, people, people, people. As we moved slowly through the mob, hand horn squawking, the dust, noise, heat, and cooking fires gave the scene a hellish aspect. Would we ever get to our hotel?

13

All three of us were, frankly, frightened . . . since that night I've known the *feel* of overpopulation.[1]

The fact is that a hot summer night on Broadway in New York or Picadilly Circus in London would put Ehrlich in the midst of a far larger crowd. Yet such an experience would not spur him to comment with grave concern about "overpopulation." On the other hand, with a little more concern and a little less fear he would have realized that what disturbed him about the crowd in Delhi was not its numbers, but its "quality"—that is, its poverty. To talk, as Ehrlich does, of "overpopulation" is to say to people: you are poor because you are too many. As this essay will show, people are not poor because they have large families. Quite the contrary: they have large families because they are poor.

Based on reasoning similar to Ehrlich's, there was a proliferation of birth control studies in the underdeveloped countries in the 1950s and 1960s. The experience of these studies is vital to our understanding the significance of the "population problem." What they share with Ehrlich is his misinterpretation of social reality: that it is the large size of the families that explains their poverty. What they share among themselves is a misinterpretation of their results: that is, if an area has a birth control program and if the birth rate in the area declines, it is concluded that the program is responsible for the decline. As we will see, the conclusion doesn't follow from the evidence. One must show that the decline in the birth rate is a result of the work of the program, and not merely coincident with it. First, let us deal with the second shortcoming: the misinterpretation of results. Later, we shall direct our attention to the misinterpretation of social reality.

One major birth control study was the Khanna Study, a study centered on a small north Indian village called

Manupur. The Khanna Study was the first birth control program to have a control as well as a test population; it is one of only three completed birth control programs that have evaluated their impact by comparing the change in the birth rates in the test population, where the program was established, with that in a control population, where no such program existed. (The almost complete absence of such studies is testimony to the *a priori* assumption of most family planners that birth control programs work.)

We shall deal with the Khanna Study in great detail in this book, but first we must briefly discuss the two other birth control field studies that included control populations: the Kyong Study and the Singur Study. The Kyong Study was begun in South Korea in 1962. It covered seven villages with a total population of 8,700 people. A control was established in seven other villages and included 12,000 people. After two years, birth rates in the test area declined by 13.2 per 1,000. However, rates in the control area declined as well: by 11 per 1,000 for the same period.[2] The speed of the decline is also revealing. In the first year of the program, rates in the test population declined by 9.7 per 1,000 and those in the control by 6.8 per 1,000. The trend was reversed in the second year, when the decline in the test population was only 3.5 per 1,000, while that in the control was 4.2 per 1,000. Without giving further analysis and supplying other—and contradictory—evidence, which the report does not do, it is not possible to attribute the decline in birth rates in the test population solely, or even primarily, to the existence of the program, which the report implies is the case. The similar decline in the control testifies that other factors must have been responsible.

The Singur Study began in West Bengal in India in 1957, and, according to the Population Council, is "generally thought to be the first successful effort to lower the birth rate in such a population through an educational program."[3] Here the decline in birth rates in the test population was almost twice that in the control, but it is still highly unlikely that this decline can be attributed to the work of the program. Table 1 shows the trend in birth rates in the test and control populations:

Table 1[4]

	Year	Births per 100 population	
		Control area	Test area
	1956	45.0	45.2
This is	1957	46.3	42.0
when the			
program	1958	45.7	42.0
began	1959	45.9	39.2
	1960	46.6	37.6
	1961	42.9	36.9

It is clear that in the period *before* the birth control program started, 1956-1957, birth rates in the test population declined by 3.2 per 1,000; yet in the four years of the program, the decline was only 5.1 per 1,000. Since the decline in birth rates began before the program did, there is no *necessary* connection between the two.

The most apparently successful of the nationwide birth control programs—programs with no control population and therefore not conducted on an experimental basis—have been those in Taiwan and South Korea. The program in Taiwan began in the Taichung area in 1962 and by 1964 included the entire island. However, during the years immediately preceding the new family planning program, fertility had already begun to decline substantially both in Taichung and Taiwan as a whole. In the period between 1959 and 1962, the crude birth rate fell by 12 percent and the general fertility rate by 9 percent in Taichung and at a somewhat lesser rate in the rest of Taiwan.[5]

Once again, the decline in the birth rate cannot necessarily be traced to the existence of the program. The experience in South Korea was much the same, since "fertility had been declining rather significantly before the start of the large-scale programs."[6] On the basis of the experience in Taiwan, one of the directors of the program wrote: "No matter how primitive he may be, man seems to have the 'rationale' to adjust his numbers in accordance with the resources available, and the environment to which he is subjected."[7]

Despite the rather less than reassuring performance "in the field," overpopulation theorists persist in their optimism and in the analysis that has led to it. One of the experts, Dudley Kirk, explains the reasons for this. While he acknowledges the general failure of birth control programs to date, he maintains his optimism: "Given the favorable attitudes found in surveys, family planning may be easier to implement than major advances in education, or the economy, which require large structural and institutional change in the society as a whole."[8]

What is important about this explanation is not only that it clarifies the *scientific* basis of the optimism—the results of the sample surveys—but that it also underlines the *political* reasons behind that same optimism: family planning is considered a *substitute* for structural and institutional change in the whole society, a change that Kirk admits is required to make advances in education or in the economy. Optimism concerning the possibility of population control without a fundamental change in the underlining social reality is, in fact, a weapon of the political conservative.

Let us turn, then, to the scientific basis for this optimism: the sample surveys, known as KAP studies. These are standardized surveys of the views of a population on the Knowledge, Aptitude, and Practice of birth control. They have been conducted by population planners in numerous countries, primarily over the last two decades. Their influence on population planners cannot be overemphasized. As one expert stated, "probably in no other field in social action has the sample survey been more widely utilized as a tool for policy formulation and program design as in family planning programs."[9]

In *Family Planning and Population Programs: A Review of World Developments*, Bernard Berelson, then vice-president of the Population Council, devoted an entire chapter to the significance of the KAP surveys. After commenting that "the sampling has been fairly good, the formulation of the questions acceptable or better, the interviewing at least adequate, and the analysis if anything overdone," he confidently concludes that "substantial proportions of people in the developing world want no more children now—from nearly a half to three-fourths." Furthermore, he tells us that this attitude can result in "a decline of . . . ten points in the birth rate of the typical developing country and a decline of one point in the growth rate."[10]

If KAP studies are so important, what have their findings been? That "*whenever asked*, substantial proportions of married couples *approve* family planning *in principle, express interest in learning* how to control their own fertility, say they *would do something* if they had appropriate means, and want the government to carry out programs along these lines."[11] But what does it mean when someone "expresses interest" in learning how to control their fertility? The uncritical acceptance of such a *general* response can only lead to misinterpretation.

A KAP survey was the basis of the Khanna Study's conclusion in the first year of its work that "nearly 90 percent [of the villagers] were in favor of contraception."[12] As we shall later see, it took years of work and persistent failure before the study staff would admit that there was a great difference in numbers between those who were in favor of contraception *in principle* and those who would accept contraceptives when offered; between those who "accepted" contraceptives and those who admitted to "using" them; and, finally, between those who said they were "using" contraceptives and those who in fact used them. Why would a villager accept contraceptives without intending to use them? And furthermore, why would they say they were using them when in fact they weren't? We shall consider all this in detail in later chapters, but, in brief, there was only one reason for such behavior: politeness. As one of the villagers explained to me: "Babuji, someday you'll understand. It is sometimes better to lie. It stops you from hurting people, does you no harm, and might even help them."

The political and scientific reasons for the emphasis on overpopulation are, in fact, two sides of the same coin. One follows from the other and the two sustain each other in a symbiotic relationship. If population control is to be a substitute for fundamental social change, then the theorist must look at the population "problem" *independently* of other aspects of social relations. It also follows that he must look at motivation as individual motivation, independent of the individual's social existence.

Let us take an example. The overpopulation theorists particularly emphasize the collection of "empirical" facts —for instance, that 30 percent of "eligible" couples reject contraception. There is nothing wrong with such a finding. What is crucial is how it is interpreted. If one understands it as an *attitude,* then the emphasis will be on the social reality in which this attitude originates. But if this finding is understood as a *fact,* stripped of its relation to other social phenomena, then the origin of this "fact" in social existence will be totally obscured, and it will be seen only in the thinking of isolated individuals. The result will be an emphasis on surveying the opinions of these individuals, as in the KAP surveys, rather than on understanding the basis of the opinions themselves in their social context. The solution will be to disseminate contraceptive devices and to "educate" individuals about the importance of using them, rather than to seek to alter the social circumstances and thus to change the social basis of the individual act.

What becomes clear is that the method of analysis in large part determines the results that follow. As important as "knowing" is the method one uses to "know." If we are to come to a true understanding of the "population problem"—one that comes to terms not only with the theoretical optimism of the "overpopulation" theorists, but also with the rather pessimistic results of the birth control programs—we need a different method. Central to this new method must be an understanding that the motivations of men and women originate in their social experience. Motivations do not exist in the abstract; their roots are to be found in a given social structure.

In the rest of the book, we will attempt an alternate understanding of the "population problem." We shall concentrate on the findings and methods of the Khanna

Study. Chapter 1 will describe the study in detail. Chapter 2 will attempt to understand the perceptions of those who formulated and executed the study, thus underlining their method of understanding the problem and their assumptions. The later chapters will seek to describe the social reality of the villagers who were the focus of the study. Our point is that the failure of the birth control program was not a failure in execution, but a failure in understanding. No program would have succeeded, because birth control contradicted the vital interests of the majority of the villagers. To practice contraception would have meant to willfully court economic disaster.

Notes

1. Paul Ehrlich, *The Population Bomb* (New York: Ballantine Books, Inc., 1968), p. 15.
2. Jae Mo Yang, "Fertility and Family Planning in South Korea," *Proceedings of the World Population Conference* (Belgrade, August 30-September 10, 1965), p. 310.
3. Population Council, "India: The Singur Study," *Studies in Family Planning* (July 1963), p. 3.
4. Ibid., p. 4.
5. Ronald Freedman, et al., *Family Planning in Taiwan, an Experiment in Social Change* (Princeton: Princeton University Press, 1969), p. 45.
6. Lien-Ping Chow, "Evaluation of the Family Planning Program in Taiwan, Republic of China," *The Journal of the Formosan Medical Association,* vol. 67, no. 9 (July 28, 1968), p. 305. See also Dudley Kirk, p. 58.
7. Ibid., p. 305.
8. Dudley Kirk, "Prospects for Reducing Natality in the Underdeveloped World," *The Annals of the American Academy of*

Political and Social Sciences, vol. 369 (January 1967), p. 59.

9. Philip M. Hauser, "Family Planning and Population Programs: A Book Review Article," *Demography,* vol. 4, no. 1 (1967), p. 402.

10. Bernard Berelson, "KAP Studies in Fertility," in *Family Planning and Population Programs: A Review of World Developments* (Chicago: University of Chicago Press, 1966), pp. 657, 659, and 658.

11. Ibid., p. 660. Emphasis mine.

12. John E. Gordon, *Exploratory Investigations I,* Population Dynamics, Chakohi Village, Punjab, India, June 1954 to March 1955, p. 277 (study report issued in October 1956). Hereafter cited as *Exploratory Investigations I.*

1

The Khanna Study

But they were so nice, you know. And they came from distant lands to be with us. Couldn't we even do this much for them? Just take a few tablets? Ah! even the gods would have been angry with us. They wanted no money for the tablets. All they wanted was that we accept the tablets. I lost nothing and probably received their prayers. And they, they must have gotten some promotion.

So Hakimjee* explained why many villagers had taken the contraceptive tablets, although they had not used them. He smiled and took another deep puff from his hand-rolled *bidi*. It was six in the morning, and several farmers squatted at the village gate listening to the Hakim tell of how the times had changed. It had rained during the night, so work would not begin till the sun was "well above the head." But now they were interrupted by a

---

*A *Hakim* is a traditional medical doctor who practices *Ayurvedic* (ancient Indian) and/or *Yunani* (ancient Arab) medicine. *Jee* is a suffix attached to a name and indicates both love and respect.

Babuji—a city gentleman of a higher social standing—who had come to stay with them for a few months.

"Aho, Aho, well said. No one will ever go back from this village saying we are not hospitable," several chimed in unison, as heads nodded in agreement.

And a young man smiled and joked, "Don't worry, Babuji. If you have any tablets, you can also give them to us. Our hearts are big." He was asked not to be so brash, for this was a matter for elders. The pride of village Manupur was at stake.

A hundred miles and six hours away from Manupur was the new and shiny capital of the state of Indian Punjab. The city had been built only a decade or so ago and had a day-after-tomorrow look about it. Sitting in a new government office, one of the two assistant field directors of the Khanna Study, Dr. Sohan Singh, reflected upon the project's unsuccessful attempt to introduce birth control in rural Punjab: "The villagers are ignorant, you know. What they need first of all is some education."[1]

Back at the Harvard School of Public Health, a fourteen-story steel and glass skyscraper in downtown Boston, the directors of the Khanna Study, seeking to explain that same failure, had written: "Westerners have strong feelings about the value of persons and of human life not necessarily shared by Punjab villagers. Some readers may feel that the pressures arising from growing numbers were self-evident. The villagers did not always hold that view."[2]

The Khanna Study—named after the market town where its field headquarters were located—was the first major field study in birth control in India. It was conducted in seven "test" villages, with a total population of 8,000 people. Its field operations lasted a total of six years, and the study cost approximately $1 million. It was a failure.

In July 1953, the Harvard School of Public Health prepared a report on the "population problem" whose thesis
was that although recent advances in the field of public
health had resulted in spectacular and welcome declines
in the death rate in "underdeveloped countries," these
very declines had generated another major problem: populations were rising at an unprecedented rate. The report
warned that "should the present trends of population
growth in several parts of the world continue unchanged
for a matter of ten or even fewer years, disastrous famine
is inevitable and civil unrest likely." Thus the prospect of
the impending "disaster" was "sufficiently real to give this
problem the same priority accorded the great plagues of
yesterday."[3]

The Harvard sponsors went on to propose a long-term
population field study aimed at devising methods that
could later be employed to control and solve the "population problem." The first step was to decide upon a location.
The state of Punjab in India, described as a major country
"suffering" from "population pressure," was selected. An
initial study report noted that the population density of
Punjab was 20 percent higher than that of the entire country. The density of District Ludhiana, which was selected
as the target area, was the highest in the Punjab, 75 percent higher than the population density of India as a
whole. Furthermore, the report noted that despite its high
concentration, the birth rate for Punjab was 40 per 1000,
the same as that of India as a whole.[4]*

The proposal found several sympathetic ears and a number of sponsors—the Rockefeller Foundation and the Indian government, in particular—which financed the field

---

*The study report gave the population density of India in 1951 as
281 per square mile; of Punjab, 338 per square mile; and of District
Ludhiana, over 500 persons per square mile.

study from 1954 to 1960 and the follow-up study in the summer of 1969. But since no contribution was made as a lump sum, the continued flow of funds was contingent upon the successful operation of the program. The study was divided into various stages, each stage acting as a control for the following one. If the findings from any stage did not justify the launching of the next, the study would be terminated. An Advisory Committee, composed of a Rockefeller Foundation representative and "leading members of the Indian medical and scientific community," was to supervise these controls and report on the progress of the study to its major donors.

The goals of the study were threefold:

1. To determine the effectiveness of a recognized method of contraception in limiting numbers of people, when applied to whole populations of rural (village) communities in a highly populated area.

2. To determine the effect of a program of family planning when offered to all members of a village community, as judged by numbers of births and deaths in that population.

3. To determine the effect of population control on health and social status.[5]

The study was originally to have four phases:

Exploratory Investigations	June 1954 to March 1955
Pilot Study	April 1955 to March 1956
Definitive Study	April 1956 to April 1960
Follow-up Study	Summer 1969

Later, another phase, Exploratory Investigations II, was added.*

---

*Exploratory Investigations I was to determine "acceptability" to the study population of both contraception in general and of a particular method or methods of contraception, for "if an affirmative

Thus three studies—Exploratory Investigations I and II, and the Pilot Study—were conducted specifically to test the level of "acceptability" of contraception among the Khanna Study population. The Definitive Study was to be launched only if the response to the offer of contraception was both affirmative and significant. Once launched, the purpose of the four-year Definitive Study would be to achieve "a significant decline" in the birth rate of the Khanna Study population.[6]

The Definitive Study was begun in April 1956 and completed in April 1960. In 1969, the Follow-up Study was conducted in the same region in order to analyze any late effects of the birth control program, and thus to gain a thorough understanding of the cumulative impact of the study.

The Follow-up Study showed that the birth control program had been a failure. Although the crude birth rate of the study population was 40 per 1000 in 1957, at the beginning of the Definitive Study, and 35 per 1000 in 1968,[7] this reduction could not be traced to the birth

---

answer to these aims were not obtained, continuation of the investigation would be purposeless" (*Exploratory Investigations I*, p. 5). Once the exploratory study was concluded, the argument was advanced to the Advisory Committee that since "observation in the village as a whole were [sic] only over a three-month period," these were "recognizably insufficient to obtain more than a strong suggestion of acceptability" and so, "a greater experience was necessary to determine the reliable level of acceptability" (*Exploratory Investigations II*, pp. 2-3). A second year-long study, Exploratory Investigations II, was therefore justified. Exploratory II was simultaneous with the Pilot Study, and both were conducted in separate villages in District Ludhiana. The aim of the Pilot Study was also "to reaffirm and refine the limits of acceptability of contraception in a village population, to get a rough measurement of the effectiveness of a simple contraceptive over a period of one year, and to justify the launching of the four-year Definitive Study" (*Pilot Study*, p. S. 1).

control program since it occurred among both the test and control populations. Instead, the decline had to be attributed to a rise in the age of marriage. The mean age of married women at first sexual union was 17.5 years in 1956, and more than 20 years in 1969.[8] In the words of the Khanna Study directors:

> Apparently the chief accomplishment of the programs for family planning had been to induce one quarter to one half of the couples *previously practicing* birth control to switch to modern methods, easier to use and more effective. The striking change in age of women at marriage is more important.[9]

Later, we shall trace this rise in the age of marriage to socioeconomic changes in the study area, but we must first turn to how the directors and staff of the study perceived the "population problem" in the Khanna area.

Notes

1. Interview with Dr. Sohan Singh (Chandigarh, Punjab, July 8, 1970).

2. John B. Wyon and John E. Gordon, *The Khanna Study: Population Problems in the Rural Punjab* (Cambridge: Harvard University Press, 1971), Preface, p. xviii. Hereafter cited as *The Khanna Study*.

3. *Original Plan of Analysis, July 1953, Part 1: Public Health Aspects*, p. 14.

4. *Exploratory Investigations I*, p. 11.

5. John E. Gordon, *First Annual Report*, December 31, 1954, p. 10.

6. *Original Plan of Analysis, July 1953, Part 3: Plan of the Study*, p. 25.

7. *The Khanna Study*, p. 300.
8. Ibid, p. 298.
9. Ibid. Emphasis mine.

2

Experience as Learning:
The Perceptions of the
Khanna Study

The continued financing of the Khanna Study was contingent on the success of its different phases. Only if the villagers were found "receptive" to the birth control program in the Exploratory and the Pilot studies would the Definitive Study be launched, a decision to be made by the Advisory Committee. Since the committee's understanding of the impact of the birth control program was based on statistical figures supplied by the study directors, the correctness of the committee's evaluation was predicated on its receiving factual and objective information. This meant that the perceptual biases of the directors would be passed on in the statistics they supplied the committee. As the analysis of these statistics included in the Appendix to this book shows, such was indeed the case. Through the figures they supplied, the directors successfully built a wall of optimism around the Advisory Committee—and around themselves—thereby exaggerating the impact of the program throughout its duration and minimizing its failure after its completion. The Advisory Committee, totally dependent for its information on the very directors whose performance it was asked to judge, was rendered super-fluous.

The purpose of the statistics the study accumulated was to find out how many of the villagers approached accepted contraceptives for use. Initially, the study simply assumed that "accepting" contraceptives was tantamount to "using" them. Such, however, was not the case. In a communication to his staff, the field director explained that "comparison of 'acceptance' with 'use' indicates that reliance on 'acceptance' probably doubles the true state of affairs." The report expresses concern that even the use rate might be exaggerated, that it "is certainly not 100 percent accurate, but it is probably of the order of 80 percent accurate."[1] If not properly qualified, the use rate was found to be seriously misleading. During the first year of the Definitive Study—from April 1956 to March 1957—although 39 percent of the fertile wives had used the foam tablets, only 8 percent had used them consistently for four months or more.[2]

Despite such disclosures late in the Definitive Study, the directors were never totally able to grasp the difference between what the villagers said they did and what they actually did. The result was that the only accurate reflection of the difference between "acceptance" and "use" was registered in the ultimate failure of the birth control program. Neither did the directors understand why the villagers were not always willing to admit verbally what was in fact the case in practice. It remains for us to understand the reasons behind this.

A person who did not accept or admitted to not using contraception was considered a "resistance" case.[3] Every "resistance" case was to be visited at least once a month—more often if the worker took the initiative and had the time. Normally, anywhere from one-half to three-quarters of an hour was spent convincing the individual of the desirability of using contraceptives. If a person "accepted" and said that she or he "used" the contraceptives, then she or he was visited twice a month, her or his supplies replenished, and data gathered. This took, on the average, about fifteen minutes for each visit. It was clearly far more agreeable for all concerned to declare oneself a "user," or even an "acceptor," rather than a "resister."

One such "acceptance" case was Asa Singh, a sometime land laborer who is now a watchman at the village high school. I questioned him as to whether he used the tablets or not:

"Certainly, I did. You can read it in their books. I didn't take them for the first few months. Then they explained to me all the advantages of using those tablets. You know, we villagers are illiterate. Well, after that, from 1957 to 1960, I never failed."

"And that's the way it is written in the book?"

"Yes, that's the way it's written in the book."

Asa Singh, however, had a son who had been born sometime in "late 1958 or early 1959." At our third meeting, I pointed this out to him and confessed I found it hard to believe his wife had been using foam tablets all the time if she had conceived a son during the same period. His face assumed a rather distant look, he scratched his beard with his forefinger; finally he looked at me and responded: "Babuji, someday you'll understand. It is sometimes better to lie. It stops you from hurting people, does you no harm, and might even help them."

"So you didn't use contraceptives?"

"That's right, I didn't. And there were several like me."

The next day Asa Singh took me to a friend's house. We went in, squatted on the floor, and sipped tea. Gradually, my eyes got used to the faint light, and I saw small rectangular boxes and bottles, one piled on top of the other, all arranged as a tiny sculpture in a corner of the room. Along with the calendar prints of gods and goddesses, movie stars, and national leaders, it decorated the room. This man had made a sculpture of birth control devices. Asa Singh said: "Most of us threw the tablets away. But my brother here, he makes use of everything."

The Khanna staff had worked in the village of Manupur for five years, on the Pilot Study as well as on the Definitive Study. It had been five years of door-to-door salesmanship, of high-pitched advertising—except that in this case the product was being given away.

The study staff had two duties: (1) to advertise the contraceptive method and convince people to use it and (2) to judge the success of its own advertising by determining the acceptance rate and, later, the use rate. The conflict between the two is quite apparent. The tendency to overestimate one's results was inherent in the duties assigned to a village worker. As Dr. Sohan Singh, the assistant field director of the study, commented, "Workers thought they would be successful workers if someone accepted. If anyone accepted, we were beaming with joy: 'One more acceptance!' People used to say birth control was written on our foreheads."[4]

Among the staff I interviewed, there was one exception to this rule. This was Banta Singh Rai: "I took the people into my confidence and didn't imply that I would be pleased if they accepted. I wasn't just interested in increasing the rate of acceptance, but wanted the truth. And you know what happened? The rate of acceptance in Manki Village was the lowest."[5] Banta Singh Rai, however, was fired midway through the study; he maintained it was because of his "low performance."

The degree of suggestion that the Khanna Study staff conveyed to the village people must have been considerable. Mrs. Rana, one of the two workers to remain throughout the study, reflected on what she termed its "innocent beginnings": "Initially, everybody just agreed with the study group and said they had the population problem."[6]

Dr. John Gordon, the study director at Harvard, wrote this entry in his diary when he first visited the villages in 1953: "Shortly, the Sirpunch joins us. He is a common man of the fields, but of a good type and all of us are impressed with him. He calls in the *Chaukidar* [the village watchman] and Taylor obtains a goodly amount of information on the village. There seems indeed to be a population problem."[7] The *First Annual Report* was able to state that "two-thirds of the villagers contributing information (20 out of 31) expressed the ideal family to be two boys and a girl."[8] Similarly, the report of Exploratory Investigations I declared: "Nearly 90 percent were in favor of contraception."[9]

Although the staff had a strong bias toward transmitting only favorable perceptions to the directors, there were occasional instances when the directors received unfavorable reports. Their response to such reports, however, was most skeptical.

From the outset, the directors and the staff had considered the "acceptance" of contraceptive tablets by a villager as tantamount to "using" them. In fact, there were many who "accepted" contraceptives not to "use" them, but to please a worker they had come to know. It was not long before the staff began to grasp this fact. Lahori Ram, one of the two workers in the Pilot Study, in a weekly report as early as June 1955, wrote that he "felt some people were bluffing" him when they accepted the contraceptives.[10] Dr. Sohan Singh, one of the two assistant field directors, maintained that by early 1956 the entire staff knew that all those who "accepted" contraceptives did not necessarily "use" them.[11] Yet it was not until December 1957, two and a half years after the first report had been made, that the directors were to admit the distinction between acceptance and use.[12] Surely, this must have provided further inducement to the proclivity the staff already had toward transmitting only favorable information to their superiors.

When the distinction between acceptance and use was finally admitted, the internal communications of the Khanna Study improved. All the members of the staff believed, as did the directors, that the initial error in misperceiving the behavior of the villagers had been rectified by this time. Yet there are good reasons to question this. The use rate that was compiled after December 1957 still relied solely on the responses of the people. It was therefore a "reactive" response, biased upward by a whole complex of psychological motivations. The ultimate failure of the Khanna Study also suggests that these rates must have been considerably inflated.

The directors (and the staff) nevertheless continued to believe that "most people want to have small families."[13] In fact, what had happened was that the gap between the perceptions of the staff and those of the directors had been removed, but there still remained a significant gap between their collective perceptions and the reality of the village.

How could these beliefs persist in the face of two facts: the use rate, even as calculated, was dipping further; and pregnancies were occurring "among users at an alarming rate."[14] The directors explained this as a short-term phenomenon,[15]* saying that the results of the Follow-up Study in 1969 would reward their efforts. They did not.

This seemingly technical difficulty—the statistical difference between acceptance and use—in fact underlines the perceptual bias of the study staff and directors. An understanding of how the staff and directors viewed and tackled the problems they faced during the operation of the study will serve to illustrate and explain further this perceptual bias.

From the outset, the Khanna Study was quite aware that it would be operating in another cultural milieu. What it feared most was the possibility of misunderstandings and misperceptions stemming from a "cultural prejudice,"[16] and precautions were taken to minimize this possibility.

The first was an attempt to "Indianize" the staff as much as possible. Dr. Carl Taylor, an American raised in India, educated at Harvard, and in 1953 a member of the medical faculty of a university in Punjab, was appointed the India director of the study, working out of the city of Ludhiana in Punjab. The field director, who bore major responsibility for the actual operation of the study, was Dr. John Wyon, who had been a medical missionary in India for nine years. The assistant field directors and the workers were all Indians—specifically, Punjabis. The only individual new to India was the study director, Dr. John Gordon. His work, however, was primarily administrative and was actually carried on from Harvard, where he spent the better part of his time.

Secondly, the study conducted a detailed investigation

---

*As the summary and conclusions on page 3 of the staff report (see note 15) state: "There is probably a big time factor which we ignore at our peril."

in the Khanna Study villages to find out the population's views on the "anatomy and physiology of [the] reproductive system,"[17] as well as studies of family life, and of attitudes toward children and sex education. The purpose was to make certain that, in so far as possible, no cultural taboos would be violated.

In fact, the study was plagued very little by the sort of "cultural" misunderstanding that it had feared in the earlier stages. What *did* plague them was the directors' basic perception of the problem. To them, overpopulation was a disease. According to the Book, *The Khanna Study,** Dr. Gordon was a pioneer in

> applying epidemiologic principles to the understanding of a variety of chronic diseases of noncommunicable origin. ... [He] was convinced that epidemiologic methods and procedures could be as usefully employed in defining the social and biological factors determining births and migrations as in analysis of the causes of disease and deaths.[18]

So far as the study was concerned, overpopulation had to be treated with the techniques of an epidemiologist, for their "value had been proven many times."[19]

From the initial 1953 *Plan of Analysis:*

> Overpopulation is a malady of society that produces wasted bodies, minds and spirits just as surely as have other familiar scourges—leprosy, tuberculosis, cancer.... [The] problem in India [is] of epidemic proportions.... Family planning lacks the spectacular elements of a peni-

---

*The Book—here and hereafter—refers to the comprehensive volume published by John B. Wyon and John E. Gordon after the completion of the Follow-up Study in 1969 and entitled: *The Khanna Study: Population Problems in the Rural Punjab* (Cambridge: Harvard University Press, 1971).

cillin. . . . The usual motivation is actual existence of tuberculosis or syphilis, or that a family has too many children.
. . . In thinking and basic knowledge of causes of different
kinds of overpopulation, the world in 1953 is in much the
same position as the pioneers of the late nineteenth century in relation to many diseases now controllable.[20]

In October 1970, in a personal interview, the director
modified this somewhat and referred to overpopulation as
a "personal disease" such as "syphilis or alcoholism or drug
addiction."[21] The inference is that "personal" diseases are
those where the patient does not know or want to know
that he is ill, but the study never admitted this. From the
outset, it found a "favorable circumstance [in] the sympathetic attitude of the local population in understanding
the need for population control."[22] When trouble arose
later, it was this assumption—that "even common people
are aware of the problem"—that was always held sacred
and never questioned. And in the Book, "excessive population pressure" was a "social malady" and the "birth control program" a "remedy."[23] The perception of overpopulation as a disease became an analytical tool for misunderstanding.

From 1954 on, the directors were "in the field." Their
perceptions had to meet the test of reality and ultimately
had to be reconciled with it. According to their own cal-
culations, the acceptance rates were dropping by 1957,
and they had to explain this unfortunate phenomenon.
Their report stated that acceptance rates were falling "primarily because local workers during the first year were less
experienced."[24] That did not, however, explain why the
rates were dipping lower as the staff became more "experienced." The first major attempts at explanation were
contained in the 1957 *Progress Report* to the Advisory
Committee and were a warning against unwarranted op-

timism in the near future. To explain the decline in the acceptance rate in the pilot village of Manupur after two years,* the *Progress Report* postulated that: "Behavior seems to follow the trend of human motivation in general: an initial enthusiasm and then a decline in interest.... it is anticipated that the forces of public health education and example in the community will lead to a gradual buildup."[25]

The difficulties, however, were not temporary; nor were these adequate explanations for the behavior of the population. As the villagers remained unreceptive to the birth control program, concern grew in the higher echelons of the staff. In late 1957, a series of proposals ensued, all designed to put an end to the apathy of the villagers. Even at this stage, with the Definitive Study half over, the major assumption—that the villagers agreed they had a population problem—was not questioned by the study directors. In the face of a rather obstinate reality, the directors resorted to some tortuous linguistic manipulations in order to sustain their optimism. One report states: "Four years of work in the India-Harvard-Ludhiana Population Study leads to the conclusion that though most village people want to have small families, they are not sufficiently motivated to make tiresome methods of birth control succeed."[26] That is to say, they are motivated, but they are not. The sincerity of the directors' convictions was faithfully echoed in the opinion held by the Advisory Committee: "The Committee agreed that over-pessimistic conclusions from the data presented are not justifiable.

---

*Manupur, after a year of the Pilot Study, was included among the seven villages that comprised the "test" population for the four-year Definitive Study.

These village people undoubtedly want to limit their families. One important problem is how much trouble they are prepared to take to achieve this end."[27]

In time, however, the directors themselves became dissatisfied with "human nature" as an adequate explanation for declining acceptance rates. And so the assistant field director, Dr. Sohan Singh, took up residence in the village of Kotla for a year. His purpose was to understand the factors that motivated the villagers to use or not use contraception. As the directors reported, this "direct field survey of reasons given by couples for not practicing contraception gave a confused impression of doubts and fears."[28] As a result, the staff was asked to improve the content and form of its communications to the villagers: they had not been given sufficient information on their own population problem to be convinced of the urgent necessity of practicing contraception; nor had this information been transmitted through the most effective channels of social communication.

What is most interesting about this analysis is the way it betrays the elitism of the social engineer: if only the "right" information can be given to the people they will be convinced; if only the leaders can be contacted and convinced, they will use their influence with the people to change their behavior. The underlying assumption is that the behavior of the population, given the environment and its constraints, is not rational: it is thus susceptible to "education." And if "education" fails, it is merely a question of not having used the right "techniques." In fact, the directors were saying that the fundamental problem lay not with the study, but with the perception the villagers had of their own environment.

Thus the field director proposed to "design an experimental unit to educate village people in demographic facts."[29] Data were to be compiled for the world, India, Punjab, District Ludhiana, Tehsil (subdistrict) Samrala, and, finally, for the villages themselves. These were to be given to the villagers to "educate" them. The formal proposal was never put into effect—it would have required, according to the study's own estimate, an initial outlay of $16,000 and much more time than the project staff had to give.

A second proposal concerned the form of communication. It was suggested that a "sketch map" of "lines of communications of ideas and attitudes" in the villages be designed[30] in order to find out who the "opinion-makers" were and then to use their authority and legitimacy to convince the villagers of the necessity of contraception. An anthropologist was hired for three months to find these "leaders" and to study the perceptions of the village people.[31]

Neither of the two proposals was new. From the very beginning, the staff had been given "demographic education" so that they could go out and convince the villagers. The only difference was that instead of "demographic education," the new proposals called it "public health education." As early as 1955, Exploratory Investigations I had proposed that the "real leaders of village opinion" be "discovered" and that "faction leaders" be "identified." The exploratory report had even emphasized that, "in retrospect, not enough time had been spent in casually visiting and chatting with such people before work began."[32] This was 1955. Now, after three years of adverse experience, the same proposal was revived. This time, too, it had little effect in salvaging the birth control program.

Gradually the objectives of the study began to change. By mid-1958, the study directors were so much on the defensive that the staff was told that its major task in the next year and a half was

1. To describe as fully and accurately as possible what village people do or do not do about family planning, and

2. To find out and describe why they act or fail to act as they do.[33]

This was no longer an "action" program oriented toward changing behavior, but one confined to the analysis and explanation of existing behavior. What ought to have been accomplished at the outset had now become the task of a failing project, halfway through its course.

It then becomes clear why, in the Book, the last two years of the birth control program are not mentioned in the text and have only one isolated reference in the Appendix. Instead, the reader is familiarized with the "communications problem,"[34] the need for the "right" demographic information, and the most effective social channels through which it must be conveyed. Two sociological explanations are then given to account for the behavior of village people—in other words, for the failure of the birth control program.

The first of these explanations is that this failure is the result of the "psychological effect of the general expectation by parents of all castes that most families are likely to lose several children." Thus if "the general experience of losing children [were] to change sharply, many more parents might become willing to practice family limitation."[35]

This was not a new idea. In fact, in 1953, the study itself had stated in a report to the Advisory Committee: "High infant mortality is a direct encouragement to fertility."[36] Stated this generally, the argument can be accepted, but this is very different from the model the directors proposed in the Book, when they argued that there would be a direct and presumably rapid response of parents to the fact of lower infant and child mortality. This directly contradicted the demographic analysis that had given rise to the Khanna Study in the first place. In 1953, in seeking to justify a birth control program in the Khanna area, where the infant mortality rate was quite high, the study directors had discussed "the effect of modern public health methods on populations through reductions of death rates,"[37] arguing that in many poor countries modern medicine has lowered the death rate, but the birth rate has not followed suit. Thus, a population problem. The report gives numerous examples—a decline in death rates in Turkey, a drastic decline in infant mortality in Guyana, neither followed by a decline in the birth rate. The pattern has been similar in India in the twentieth century, where death rates have declined much faster than birth rates. The point here is that a reduction in deaths— general or infant—does not necessarily bring about a reduction in the birth rate. The directors were resurrecting in 1971 an argument they had shot down in 1953.

The infant mortality hypothesis also assumes that most of the Khanna Study population overestimates its infant mortality rate and thus has a higher number of *surviving children than it really wants*. This only sustains the study's central assumption, that the villagers recognize they have a population problem.

The fact is that an overwhelming majority of the people in the Khanna Study area have a large number of children not because they overestimate their infant mortality rates, but because they want *larger* families. More important, they want them because they *need* them.

The second sociological explanation for the failure of the program was given by Dr. Gertrude Woodruff, a social anthropologist hired by the Khanna Study. Dr. Woodruff sought to "demonstrate the influence of net emigration on restraining local population growth."[38] Her argument went thus: in the years 1957 to 1959, the demographic statistics for the Khanna Study population were as follows:

Birth rate	38 per 1000
Death rate	17 per 1000
Rate of natural increase	21 per 1000
Net emigration	11 per 1000
Net population growth	10 per 1000

It was therefore clear that the villagers were managing to solve a substantial part of their "population problem" by emigration.[39] It was true, as the data gathered by the Khanna Study itself showed, that over 25 percent of the families in the village were supplementing their income by sending a son away to send some money back.[40] In fact, many families had specifically educated one son solely so that he would later emigrate and help supplement the family income. But if the villagers were solving a substantial part of their "population problem" by emigrating, they were clearly finding a cure for a problem after it had arisen. And if this was the case, then they should have been receptive to the offer of contraception because it would *prevent* the "population problem." But they were not. The reality was that these villagers were solving their *poverty* problem by having larger families: most of them use the labor of their children within the village, and over a quarter of the families resort to emigration to supplement their family income. This alone explains their lack of receptivity to contraception.

The emigration situation, moreover, was changing. When the village economy expanded and became more productive through partial mechanization of agriculture, the net emigration dropped from 11 per 1000 (in 1959) to

5.5 per 1000 (in 1969). The sons who had previously gone away now stayed home, for the work had increased and they were needed in the village. In 1969, as in 1959, they were an asset to the family—in one case by emigrating, in the other by not. In both cases they earned and were indispensible.

Emigration in the Khanna Study villages was a socioeconomic variable, not a demographic one. To graph the significance of emigration, we must go beyond the statistics and identify the social classes that were most likely to resort to it. We shall return to this later.

Limiting reference to the birth control program to an abridged statement of its performance could not conceal its failure. The program had failed to reduce the birth rates, and that failure is only marginally alluded to in the Book. In a final effort to legitimize this, the Book goes so far as to change the very goals of the study so that they may be more consonant with its performance.

The reader will recall that the goals of the study, as defined in 1954, were general and conditional:

1. To determine the effectiveness of a recognized method of contraception in limiting numbers of people, when applied to whole populations of rural (village) communities in a highly populated area.

2. To determine the effect of a program of family planning when offered to all members of a village community, as judged by numbers of births and deaths in that population.

3. To determine the effect of population control on health and social status.[41]

The purpose of the Exploratory and the Pilot studies, a work of two years, was to determine the "limits of acceptability of contraception in a village population."[42] It was clearly stated that "if an affirmative answer to these aims were not obtained, continuation of the investigation would be purposeless."[43] This was the function of the controls. Had the findings of these studies been negative, one could not have called the Khanna Study a failure. At this stage, it was essentially a demographic inquiry.

Once the Definitive Study was launched in 1956, however, the goals of the study changed significantly. Its orientation was now no longer toward inquiry, but toward performance. This had been clearly specified as early as 1953, in the *Plan of the Study* that accompanied the request for funds submitted to the Rockefeller Foundation and the government of India. Assuming that the Exploratory and the Pilot studies would justify the launching of the Definitive Study, the *Plan* stated:

> The experiment will have succeeded fully if at the end of the observations *a significant decline* in birth per 100 woman-years of village population can be demonstrated as a result of induced contraceptive measures; and that significant changes toward health and social status exist in experimental villages compared with controls.[44]

The *Statement of the Project,* sent to the same two donors, clarified this further: "The conclusions reached in the course of the studies are intended as a basis for administrative programs at the provincial or national level, with the intent of limiting general populations."[45] And yet, in 1971, the Book stated: "The Khanna Study had two primary objectives: to study population dynamics and the numerous influences that account for variations in population numbers, and to measure the results of an instituted program for birth control."[46] The Preface of the Book states: "This book describes an eight-year prospective field study of population dynamics in rural India. . . ."[47]

The Book depicts the Khanna Study as a demographic inquiry. In fact, it was a birth control program.

A lot had changed in the translation of the goals from 1954 to 1971. It was essentially a pragmatic translation. The areas in which the directors thought they had succeeded—in the study of population dynamics and the various influences that affect the variations in population numbers—became the primary objectives of the study, although they had not even been among the three goals stated in 1953 or the two specified at the beginning of the Definitive Study. The area in which they had failed—the birth control program—became a secondary goal. What had been the third goal in 1954 (and also one of the two stated aims of the Definitive Study)—to determine the effect of population control on health and social status— was not mentioned in 1971. Needless to say, such an effect could not be measured since the Khanna Study had failed to achieve its precondition: population control. What was in 1954 a statement of purpose became in 1971 a reminder of failure. So just as the birth control program was reduced to a secondary goal, this third goal was consigned to oblivion.

The perceptual bias of the study thus turned out to be not the cultural or national bias that the directors had at the outset viewed as the greatest potential danger in successfully conducting their field work. The content of their bias was not only more specific but also different.

At the time of its full operation, the Khanna Study had a field staff of twenty. I was able to interview eleven of them, and I asked each why he or she thought the village population had not been receptive to the birth control program. Each usually offered several answers, but one clearly predominated. Nine of the eleven responded that the villagers were either "illiterate" or "prejudiced" or that they needed some "basic education" or "demographic education." Underlying these answers, and sometimes stated explicitly, was the insistence that the villagers had acted out of ignorance. A typical response came from Dr. Prem Vir Ghulati, a supervisor of male field workers: "Education is the answer and illiteracy the curse. I keep on telling my supervisors: India's population problem will only be solved if we give some basic education to our people."[48]

In the final analysis, there was little difference in the perceptions of the directors and the staff, of the American members and the Indian members of the Khanna Study. Except for two staff members, no one was willing to admit that the Khanna villagers might be acting rationally.

The study had misplaced its fears of acting out of a cultural bias. All efforts had been expended to ensure that the field workers were all Punjabis and that the American supervisors had considerable familiarity with India. But the staff, though Punjabis like the villagers, were all members of the urban, educated middle class. What they shared with the directors was a *bourgeois* culture. What plagued the study was not a *national* (Western vs. Indian) bias but a *class* bias. This bias pervaded its staff as well as its directors, without distinction of race, religion, or "culture."

Notes

1. *Use of contraceptives in seven Punjab villages, April 1955 to March 1958*, p. 2 (staff report for the India-Harvard-Ludhiana Population Study, issued May 6, 1958).
2. *Agenda* for the sixth Advisory Committee meeting of the India-Harvard-Ludhiana Population Study (March 21, 1959), p. 5.

3. Interviews with Mrs. Sampuran Singh Ghuman (Ranjeet Bagh, Punjab, August 14, 1970) and Pandit Lahori Ram (Jallunder City, Punjab, August 6, 1970).

4. Interview with Dr. Sohan Singh (Chandigarh, Punjab, July 8, 1970).

5. Interview with Mr. Banta Singh Rai (Amritsar, Punjab, August 7, 1970).

6. Interview with Mrs. Kulwant Rana (Khanna, Punjab, July 8, 1970).

7. *Original Plan of Analysis, July 1953, Part 6: Extracts from Dr. Gordon's Diary*, p. 134.

8. *First Annual Report*, December 31, 1954, p. 55.

9. *Exploratory Investigations I*, p. 277.

10. Interview with Pandit Lahori Ram (August 6, 1970).

11. Interview with Dr. Sohan Singh (July 8, 1970).

12. *Use of contraceptives in seven Punjab villages, April 1955 to March 1958*, p. 2 (staff report).

13. John B. Wyon, *Need for an effort to increase the strength of desire of Punjab people to achieve small families*, p. 4 (staff report, April 11, 1958).

14. *Use of contraceptives during the first year of offer in seven Punjab villages up to March 1958*, p. 4 (staff report issued July 16, 1958).

15. *Use of contraceptives in seven Punjab villages, April 1955 to March 1958* (staff report).

16. *Original Plan of Analysis, July 1953, Part 1: Public Health Aspects*, p. 13; *Progress Report, 1955*, p. 3; *Exploratory Investigations I*, p. 218; *The Khanna Study*, p. 3; Interview with Dr. John B. Wyon (November 12, 1970).

17. *Exploratory Investigations I*, pp. 218-250.

18. *The Khanna Study*, p. 3.

19. Ibid., p. 4.

20. *Original Plan of Analysis, July 1953, Part 2: The Epidemiologic Approach*, pp. 8-21.

21. Interview with Dr. John Gordon (Cambridge, Mass., October 26, 1970).

22. *Original Plan of Analysis, July 1953, Part 4: Statement of the Project*, p. 4.

23. *The Khanna Study*, p. 18.

24. John E. Gordon and John B. Wyon, *A field study of motivation to family planning*, p. 4 (staff report, no date).
25. John E. Gordon, *Progress Report, April 1957*, p. 2.
26. *Need for an effort to increase the strength of desire of Punjab people to achieve small families*, p. 8 (staff report).
27. *Minutes* of the Advisory Committee meeting (October 29, 1957), p. 3.
28. *The Khanna Study*, p. 47.
29. John B. Wyon, *Design of a special study to determine factors which influence the decision of village people to use or not to use contraceptives*, p. 3 (staff report, July 4, 1957).
30. Ibid.
31. *Proposed field work for anthropologist in Chakohi: July to September 1959* (staff report, July 19, 1959).
32. *Exploratory Investigations I*, p. 36.
33. *Use of contraception during the first year of offer in seven Punjab villages up to March 1958*, p. 6 (staff report).
34. *The Khanna Study*, Chs. 9 and 10.
35. Ibid., p. 200.
36. *Original Plan of Analysis, July 1953, Part 2: The Epidemiologic Approach*, p. 35.
37. *Original Plan of Analysis, July 1953, Part 1: Public Health Aspects*, pp. 8-13.
38. *The Khanna Study*, p. 48.
39. Ibid., p. 226.
40. Ibid.
41. *First Annual Report*, December 31, 1954, p. 10.
42. *Pilot Study* (issued in November 1958), p. S. 1.
43. *Exploratory Investigations I*, p. 5.
44. *Original Plan of Analysis, July 1953, Part 3: Plan of the Study*, p. 25. Emphasis mine. The same statement, word for word, was given to the Advisory Committee in the *Progress Report up to 1954*.
45. *Original Plan of Analysis, July 1953, Part 4: Statement of the Project*, p. 1.
46. *The Khanna Study*, p. 277.
47. Ibid., Preface, p. xvii.
48. Interview with Dr. Prem Vir Ghulati (New Delhi, August 14, 1970).

3

Technology
and Social Structure

Members of the Khanna Study came to the conclusion that it was primarily out of ignorance that the villagers had rejected the offer of contraceptive technology; their solution was some kind of education. This implies a similar obstinacy to all other forms of technological change in the study population.* Yet, as the experience of one of the study villages—Manupur—shows, such was not the case: in fact, in this century, life in Manupur has been radically altered by a series of far-reaching technological changes. The pace of change was very slow in the first half of the century, gathered momentum in the 1950s, and was particularly rapid in the 1960s. A historical examination of

---

*Our discussion here concerns the *general* acceptance of *technology* as opposed to the *specific* acceptance of *technique*. Admittedly, the resistance to the adoption of a technique can be very different in the case of economic technology (e.g., tractors) from that in the case of personal technology (e.g., contraceptives). In talking of technology, as opposed to technique, however, it is possible to equate economic with personal technology. The point is that a people will be receptive to a form of technology (any technology) only if they stand to benefit from its introduction.

the pace of technological change reveals an intimate relationship between this process and the changing social structure in the village. Only under certain social conditions—that is, only when the adoption of a particular technology was in their interest—were the people responsive to technological change. The purpose of this chapter is to understand the social basis of technological change historically.

The primary impact of British rule on the Punjab* was the creation of conditions highly favorable to the existence of a moneylending class. Before the British colonization of the Punjab, debt was common, but the moneylender was not powerful.[1] In the first place, land was owned collectively by the peasants in the village, and without private property, alienation from the land was not possible. Secondly, the state appropriated most of the agricultural surplus as revenue, leaving little for a moneylender to thrive on. Finally, the moneylender had little "outside" assistance since the state was most apathetic to the rights of the creditor.

British control of the Punjab was firmly established by 1849. The first important act of the colonial government was legally to establish individual property rights over land. The peasants who cultivated the land now became its owners or proprietors. This was the beginning of in-

---

*The state of Punjab lies in the northwest of the Indian subcontinent. At independence, it was divided between India and Pakistan; today it is an Indian state bordered on the west by Pakistan, on the north by the Himalayan mountains and the state of Kashmir, while the south lies in the Rajasthan Desert. The land of Punjab is a fertile plateau which forms a part of the great Indo-Gangetic Plain, stretching from the Hindu Kush Mountains of Afghanistan to the hills of Assam on the Burmese border. The Khanna Study took place in District Ludhiana in central Punjab.

heritance; it was also the beginning of the problem of the subdivision of land.

The colonial government also imposed a land tax, known as the "land revenue system." The revenue officers were instructed by the state to collect a third of the peasant's yearly gross produce as tax. This was later reduced to a fourth and finally to a sixth. Theoretically, the tax was assessed by the state upon the entire village for a number of years. In fact, the village headman or village representatives were responsible for the payment and assigned a specific quota to each cultivator.[2] But more important than the amount of the tax, for the peasant, was its rigidity. Regardless of the nature of the harvest, of whether there was rain or drought, a specific payment had to be made twice a year.[3] Given the fragmentation of land, one small drought was enough to drive an average peasant into debt. Not only that, but the tax had to be paid in cash. To obtain money for his crops, the peasant was obliged to sell them to the grain dealer—who was also the moneylender.

The position of the moneylender was further strengthened by the legal system established by the colonial administration. Civil law, in recognizing contractual rights of the creditor over the debtor, favored the literate creditor over the illiterate debtor. The law governing "the simplest of contracts—a loan, lease, or mortgage—had now become so complicated that all such cases had to be referred to the professional advisers."[4]* The peasant was thus at the mercy of the moneylender, the grain dealer,

---

*Thus, for instance, under the Easement Act of 1882, if a villager had a familiar pathway closed to his ancestral field, he had to be told in English—translation into any language, with or without a literature, being impossible—that he must sue "the deminant [sic] owner for a release of the servient heritage under Chapters IV and V of the Easement Act."

and the petition writer. All three professions were usually combined in a single individual: in Manupur this was the *Brahmin.**

The British system had two important consequences for society in Manupur. While precolonial India was no paradise, the development of inequalities in Manupur are the direct result of a colonial policy which gave rise to the private ownership of land—and thus, to a market in land —and subsequently to a labor market. It was also largely upon the provisions of the colonial system that the dominance of the Brahmin moneylender rested. With the famines of 1860-61 and 1869, and the heavy mortality among cattle, the rule of the village moneylender was secured. Moneylending gradually became the most profitable occupation in the province.† The 1868 Punjab census listed 53,263 bankers and moneylenders in the province. By 1911, their numbers had risen to 193,890, a ratio of 1:100 for the population.‡ To say the least, the Punjab— urban and rural—was ridden with moneylenders.

It is important to realize that the moneylender had lit-

---

*In the traditional caste system—i.e., the social division of labor spelt out by the ancient *Vedas*—the Brahmins were envisioned as the priestly and clerical caste. In colonial Manupur, however, their social position was the product of both religious and economic dominance.

†In 1917-18, 1 percent of the Punjab population was moneylenders, while 30.04 percent were engaged in other trades, the public service, and industries. Yet the tax assessed on moneylenders was 740,000 rupees out of the total 3.7 million rupees, and their income was 35 million rupees out of 75 million (see Calvert, pp. 129-130).

‡In the whole of India, excluding the Punjab, the proportion of moneylenders to the total population was 1:367. Although the population of the Punjab was only one-eleventh that of India, a quarter of all moneylenders found in British India in 1911 resided and worked in the Punjab (for all statistics, see Calvert, pp. 129-130).

tle desire to own the land, for proprietory rights yielded little profit. As "a purchaser of the land, he got only the land, but as mortgagee he got the land and a hardworking submissive *owner-tenant* as well."[5]* The mortgagor in the Punjab was considered an owner-tenant and was entered in the records as a tenant. To get an idea of the power of the moneylender, one only has to look at the figures. In 1875-76, 44 percent of the cultivated land in rural Punjab was held by farmers who had become tenants; by 1918-19, the figure had risen to over 51 percent.

The peasants in Manupur were no exception to this trend. By village estimates, after World War I well over half the owner-cultivators had at least some of their land mortgaged to the moneylenders. Under them existed a stratum of landless agricultural laborers. Together the two formed about 75 percent of the total population of Manupur, both dominated by the Brahmin moneylenders, a parasitic stratum contributing little to the productive economy of the village.

---

*A number of facts should be emphasized here. First, as Calvert reports (p. 87), "The mortgagor is, in the great majority of cases, entered in the records as tenant cultivating under the mortgagee," that is, as an owner-tenant. Secondly, the "area [of land] sold was generally half of that mortgaged." In 1871, "in Gurdaspur 66.5 percent of the mortgages were made to moneylenders but only 37 percent of sales," which was "further evidence that the moneylenders were anxious to secure the produce of the land without assuming the responsibility of ownership." And finally, "the mortgages were mostly taking place in districts known to be prosperous and were in favor of moneylenders and that the lands so encumbered were the most fertile; while the sales were in precarious districts and were mostly in favor of other agriculturalists" (Calvert, p. 126). District Ludhiana lay in the first category, and its peasants were primarily those who had mortgaged their lands to the moneylenders; that is, they were owner-tenants.

It should be no surprise that under these circumstances the peasants—and particularly the owner-tenants, who formed the majority of the cultivators—had little motivation for improving their agricultural methods and raising the productivity of the land. As agricultural prices increased, the increasing power of the moneylender was reflected in the gradual change from cash rents to rents in kind. If the peasant were to improve his farming methods and increase his productivity, the moneylender would simply demand a larger share of the produce. As H. Calvert, registrar of the Cooperative Societies in Punjab in 1920, noted:

> These tenants generally take less care in preparing the land for crops, plough it less often, manure it less and use fewer implements upon it than owners. They grow less valuable crops, especially avoiding those requiring the sinking of capital in the land; they make little or no effort at improving their fields; they keep a lower type of cattle; they avoid perennials and bestow no care on trees.[6]

Agricultural production in such a society was particularly susceptible to the vicissitudes and vagaries of nature. Too much or too little rain or sun was enough to plunge the farmer still further into debt. A slightly delayed harvest had the same effect. To the outsider the system seemed most irrational—that is, inimical to the interests of the majority of the people in the village. And yet the peasant in Manupur was most rational: regardless of how "beneficial" any form of agricultural technology was in the abstract, he realized that the benefits went to the moneylender, not the tiller. And it thus happened that the most radical technological departures in Manupur in the first half of the century were those that benefited the Brahmin aristocracy. The innovations introduced into Manupur in the 1920s and 1930s were the radio, the handpump, the watch, and the bicycle, and their ownership was confined to the three leading Brahmin families. Significantly, these technological changes were on the side of consumption, not production; were external to the agricultural sector; and were, in their context, luxury items.

Agricultural technology changed only slightly. At the beginning of the century, the peasants tilled the land with simple tools. Gradually the wooden cartwheel gave way to the iron wheel, and the wooden plough became a relic of the past. The substitution of iron for wood soon embraced all agricultural tools except the roller used to level the earth. The most important change was in the method of watering the fields, as the old leather-bucket system gave way to the Persian wheel, making it possible to get a larger quantity of water in a steady stream. The wooden handle of the Persian wheel was pulled by a camel supervised by a child. When a camel was not available, as was often the case, the same work was accomplished by several children working together. The source of energy for this technology was confined to the people or the animals they owned. But the Persian wheel affected only a minority of peasant farms. (Even in 1955, when the Khanna Study came to Manupur, only a quarter of the fields in the village had Persian wheels.) The modern machine had not yet come to Manupur.

The minority who owned the Persian wheel were those cultivators who had not yet mortgaged their land to the moneylenders. Even when capital was externally available, it made little sense for the tenants to invest in the land.*

---

*As early as 1813, beginning in those parts of India it already controlled, the colonial government had offered to advance capital to the peasants to relieve them of the necessity of resorting to the village

As long as the peasant producer remained subservient to the moneylender, and the moneylender reaped the rewards of increased productivity, the system remained highly resistant to technological innovation. For technological change to take place on the side of production, it was necessary that the producing classes be free from the grip of the parasitic moneylenders. A dynamic economy was not possible without a dynamic dominant class.

The position of the Brahmin aristocracy has declined in the last two decades, gradually but completely. The initial blow was struck in 1937 when the Punjab government passed a law that canceled any debts where interest payments had at least doubled the principal.* (According to the grandson of the richest moneylender in Manupur, "the largest part of the money was given to the farmers by my grandfather and we had received at least three times the amount."[7]) This law canceled most of the debts in Manupur, but did not get to the root of the problem. The failure of a single harvest was sufficient to drive farmers

---

bankers for loans. These efforts were later extended to the Punjab. They failed because the peasants were already indebted to the moneylenders, and because, as Col. W. G. Davies, commissioner of Delhi, admitted to the Famine Commission of 1878-79: ". . . there was always before them the knowledge that they might have to pay a higher rent if they sank a well or otherwise increased the productivity of the land, and this knowledge essentially had the effect of permanently checking any disposition on their part to lay out money in improvement" (from *Punjab Report in Reply to the Enquiries Issued by the Famine Commission*, 2 [1878-79], p. 592; quoted in Chhabra, pp. 177-178).

*The law was passed at the height of anti-British nationalist resistance. The movement had incorporated the demands of the tenants in the Punjab.

with small holdings back into debt,* and the Brahmin was still the only financier in Manupur.

In July 1949, as part of a statewide reform, the Punjab government established a Cooperative Society in Manupur. Its purpose was to lend money to the cultivators at a relatively low interest rate, 9.5 percent, as compared to the 20-30 percent rate the moneylenders usually charged. As a matter of policy, however, the society gave only "clean" loans—to farmers who were not in debt. Few qualified. So although the Cooperative Society established a competing source of capital, in practice it was only of marginal importance.

In 1960, District Ludhiana was selected as one of the seven model districts in India where the Intensive Agricultural Development Program (IADP) was to be established. The IADP centered around the Cooperative Society, which has two branches, the Primary Society and the Land Mortgage Bank. The more important is the Primary Society, and it was here that the major change was instigated. The Primary Society loaned money to *any* member cultivator, and a farmer had to fulfill only two conditions to become a member: he had to own land and pay the necessary dues. To become a life member of the Primary Society, a cultivator had to pay 111 rupees; by 1970, 98 percent of all farmers were members. Loans from the IADP could only be used for the purchase of a tubewell, chemical fertilizers, wheat seeds, or for repaying any past debts.†

---

*See Chapter 4: nearly half the farmers in Manupur had small land parcels.

†For information pertaining to the IADP, I am indebted to the secretary of the Primary Society, Sardar Malkiet Singh Sekhon.

The Land Mortgage Bank makes loans up to 30,000 rupees for buying a tractor, a tubewell, or freeing land from private debt. Life membership costs 105 rupees and is also open only to those who possess land. The Bank has fifty farmers (about 30 percent) as members. Its loans are repayable in five to ten years, and are given at 9 percent interest. Land is taken as a pledge and interest deducted from its yearly yields.

It is the IADP that has acted as the single most important agency for bringing change in the social structure of Manupur. Loans were granted to farmers both for repaying their debts and for making changes in agricultural production. By providing a source of financing independent of the Brahmin moneylenders, the Cooperative Society successfully undermined the material basis of the Brahmin aristocracy. The cultivator-owners, about 60 percent of the population, have now become its dominant class.* The effect of the change in the social structure on the nature of the technology used in Manupur is clearly discernible.

There remained, however, one significant hindrance to the success of the IADP in Manupur: this was the small size of the typical landholding. Since the average farm was only about six acres, the gain in productivity from partial mechanization was usually not sufficient to justify its expense. Thus although elements of the new agricultural technology were introduced in the 1950s, their spread was not possible until well over a decade later.

Part of the answer to this problem came in 1967, when a new variety of wheat was introduced. It was called

---

*There exists significant differentiation within this class, which will be discussed in the next chapter.

Kalyan—prosperity—and, as a result, wheat yields often trebled. Though priced at 1 rupee* per kilogram on the market when they first appeared, the seeds, according to the farmers, were selling at nearly 100 rupees per kilogram the following year. Even so, the area under wheat cultivation increased from 22 percent in 1960-61 to over 60 percent in 1969-70.[8]

The significance of the new seed was that it increased the productivity of all land, including the small holdings. The end result was a far-reaching change in agricultural technology. The tubewell quickly replaced the Persian wheel and the drilled well. The highest loan the Primary Society gave was 4,000 rupees, the price of a tubewell, and by 1970, 75 percent of the farmers had taken a loan to purchase their tubewells.

Most of the wells that had been used to draw drinking or cleaning water fell into disuse; instead, every house began to have its own hand waterpump. The demand for chemical fertilizers also increased. By 1970, there was not one farmer who did not use chemical fertilizers. Animal manure was now used only as a supplement. Farmers who had for many years used a handcutter to make fodder for cattle now found it desirable to save both their time and labor by investing in a mechanical chaffcutter.

In 1964, the village was electrified. Tubewells and chaffing machines could now be operated by electrical motors. By 1970, there were 127 tubewells run by oil engines. Of these, 35 also had electrical motors. Farmers owning

---

*Up to 1967, $1.00 was equivalent to 4.75 rupees at the official exchange rate. In 1967, Mrs. Gandhi's government devalued the rupee. As a result, $1.00 fetched 7.50 rupees at the official exchange rate.

numerous cattle (usually meaning more than six)—33 percent of all farmers—electrified their chaffing machines.

Such a significant change in the agricultural technology of a rural society was bound to have wide repercussions. Agriculture became an increasingly "scientific" activity. Fertilizers had to be put in in specific amounts at particular times of the year. The watering of the fields had to be strictly regulated. The electrical motor or the oil engine operating the tubewell and the chaffing machine gave a specific output for a given unit of time, and also cost a specific amount of money. Wheat was marketed, and several farm and household necessities purchased, in the nearby town of Khanna. But there, shops opened and closed at specific hours. All this meant a greater emphasis upon time, for time had become money. No wonder the watch, bought by only a few Brahmins in the 1920s and 1930s, proliferated among the agricultural classes in the village in the 1960s.

Attitudes toward the outside world also changed, for the outside world was now the source of the new prosperity. For instance, in 1969 and again in 1970, wheat yields declined slightly. In 1950, such a disaster would have meant the gods were angry, and the solution would have been prayers and offerings. To be sure, there were prayers in 1970, too, but they were not emphasized. The crucial change was to the now widely held belief that the problem was susceptible to a human, "scientific," solution. As one farmer said to me:

> I have heard on the radio that there is a certain deficiency of salts in the soil. But, they have cautioned us to wait until the experiments are complete in the Agricultural University [at Ludhiana]. You see, they are not absolutely sure as yet. The moment I get a "go" from them [on the radio], I shall get zinc and ferrous sulphate from

the Cooperative Society or Khanna and sprinkle the soil with it.

Changes in the agricultural technology meant increased contacts with the outside world, and this in turn resulted in a change in communications technology. In Manupur, this meant the proliferation of the bicycle and the radio, among cultivators as well as merchants. In 1970, almost 75 percent of the families in Manupur owned at least one bicycle, and nearly 24 percent of the families had at least one radio in the house.

The "new" technology also spread to the nonagricultural sector, but to only those aspects of it controlled by the wealthiest cultivators; it thus benefited from their prosperity. A flour mill, operated by a diesel engine, was set up in Manupur in 1950. In 1964, the diesel engine was replaced by an electric motor. Another mill, also run by electricity, was set up in 1966. The sewing machine began to appear among the cultivator families.

The products of technology that made the least impact on Manupur were those that can be called semiluxury or luxury items. Six households (1.8 percent) owned electric irons and another thirty (9.0 percent) used irons heated by coal. But since these were the prosperous families of the men who had the most frequent contact with the nearby towns, men who were thus expected—or wanted— to set certain standards, these were not luxury items in their context. The teacher and the clerk were expected to wear ironed clothes to work. The prosperous farmer and the trader would not be respected unless they emulated the ways of the town when visiting it for business purposes. The least-adopted form of technology was the ceiling or table fan. It was truly a luxury item: its possession could only be boasted of by twenty-six (8 percent) of the village families, those of the most prosperous farmers—a rural bourgeoisie in the making, a supposed testimony to the success of the IADP.*

Once having severed their material dependence on the Brahmins, the farmers (Jats) did not just stop at advancing their immediate interests—through introducing new technologies in production and consumption—but also went on to secure their independence in less material realms of social life. Ramswaroop, an elderly Brahmin in his fifties, commented on the radical change in Manupur:

> [Once] only Brahmins performed priestly functions. The Jats couldn't even begin to move the plough until the Brahmin had performed certain rituals. Then, we were held in esteem and needed. Now, Jats say they are not Hindus and don't believe in our rituals.

When free from the material domination of the Brahmins, it became possible for the Jat farmers to proclaim

---

*It should be emphasized that while the creation of the Cooperative Society in 1949 was part of an India-wide reform, the introduction of the IADP in 1960 was confined to only seven model districts. Significantly, the social structure in Manupur in 1960 was radically different from that in most of contemporary rural India, where social relations remain primarily semifeudal and landlordship exists as a major problem. (For a short and excellent summary of social relations in contemporary rural India, see Charles Bettelheim, *India Independent* [New York: Monthly Review Press, 1968], pp. 177-200, 215-220.) Even if the IADP were to be extended to the rest of India, and low-interest capital thus made accessible to the peasantry, the tenant-farmers would have little motivation to improve the technical basis of agricultural production. The monetary gains from any such improvement would be the preserve of the landlord, not his tenants. Under such circumstances, one prerequisite to increasing the level of agricultural technology is structural change, specifically in the pattern of land ownership. This would be tantamount to carrying through a social revolution.

their religious independence. A fundamental change in the material aspect of social relations made possible corresponding changes in other aspects of social relations.

Notes

1. The historical information in this section is based primarily on the following readings: H. Calvert, *The Wealth and Welfare of the Punjab: Being Some Studies in Punjab Rural Economics* (Lahore, 1922), pp. 120-139; G. S. Chhabra, *Social and Economic History of the Punjab (1849-1901)* (Jallunder City: S. Nagin & Co., 1962), pp. 168-198, 301-334; Romesh Dutt, *The Economic History of India in the Victorian Age, 1837-1900,* vol. 2 (first publication 1903; second publication 1960, by the Ministry of Information and Broadcasting, Government of India), pp. 60-72; and H. K. Trevaskis, *The Land of the Five Rivers: An Economic History of the Punjab from the Earliest Times to the Year of the Grace 1890* (Oxford: Oxford University Press, 1928), pp. 307-350.
2. Dutt, p. 71.
3. Chhabra, p. 322.
4. Chhabra, p. 326; quoting a British administrator, S. S. Thorburn, from *Mussalmans and Moneylenders in the Punjab* (1886), pp. 246-247.
5. Calvert, p. 126. Emphasis mine.
6. Ibid., pp. 92-93.
7. Correspondence with Shri Shaktiprasad (December 26, 1970).
8. The 1960 figures are from *The Khanna Study,* p. 304. The 1969-70 figures are village estimates.

4

The Population Problem and the Agricultural Classes

In the post-1946 independence period, Manupur was the focus of two major programs designed to alleviate the poverty of the Indian countryside and attack what were considered the two primary reasons for the low level of material development in rural India. The first program, which we described in the last chapter, was designed to tackle the problem of lack of capital. The second was designed to solve the problem of "overpopulation." Its agent was the Khanna Study. It failed,* and we turn now to an explanation of the reasons for that failure, reasons which can only be understood in terms of caste and class.

---

*After the completion of the Khanna Study in 1960, the Indian government established a birth control clinic in the study villages in 1963. As the final analysis undertaken by the Khanna Study in 1969 demonstrated, the activities of this clinic also failed: "Apart from a few couples who adopted one or other of the modern methods, practice of birth control in 1969 seemed much the same as in 1959. . . . The collected data apparently reflect little growth in a conviction of benefits from fewer children" (*The Khanna Study,* pp. 297-298).

This chapter will discuss the agricultural classes. We will attempt to understand the material conditions of their existence, the importance of the size of the work force in their work, and the influence of those two factors on the size of the agricultural family.

The traditional Punjabi village was by and large a self-sufficient community. Its economy was based on land, and a majority of the population worked either as owner-cultivators, tenant-owners, or farm laborers. A significant minority were in "service" occupations: smithery, carpentry, water carrying, etc.

The allocation of labor to the various occupations was determined by birth: caste determined occupation. A child born into a specific caste inherited the corresponding occupation. The name of the different castes—as is still the case in Manupur—are the names of the different occupations. All members of the village community—whether Sikh, Hindu, or Muslim—belonged to a specific caste. In this sense, caste was a traditional *Indian* institution, one that applied to more than just Hindu society.*

The social hierarchy in the village was a caste hierarchy, with each caste having a specific status. There were "high" and "low" castes, with further delineations among them.

---

*Caste is usually understood in terms of the Vedic *Varna* (color) system as it appeared in the *Manusmriti*, which views society as comprised of major castes: *Brahmin, Kshatriya, Vaishya, Shudra,* and, finally, the outcaste *Achuta*. With the work of anthropologist M. N. Srinivas (*Caste in Modern India* [Bombay: Asia Publishing House, 1962], pp. 63-69), most anthropologists have come to accept the *Jati* (Sanskrit: who is born), the thousands of endogamous communities representing the localized manifestation of caste, as the fundamental unit in Indian society and thus as a realistic definition of caste. For the purpose of this book, caste and *Jati* should be considered as being synonymous.

Life, marriage, and friendship took place within caste boundaries. Occupation, income, and status were inter-related. Membership within a caste also specified place of residence, manner of speech, and style of dress and orna-mentation. To belong to a caste was thus to behave in a customary way. Contacts between members of different castes were along lines of socially accepted behavior, and rules of pollution and purity played a significant role. An individual was taught and expected to give deference to those "higher" in the world of caste, and to legitimately expect the same from those whose status was "lower" than his. The world of caste was a world of institutionalized inequality.

The Khanna Study took place in seven villages in District Ludhiana in the state of Punjab. The market town of Khanna, with an estimated population of over 20,000, lies a little over twenty miles down the Grand Trunk Road (of Kipling fame) from Ludhiana to Delhi. To get to Manupur, a visitor must take a *tempoo** for two miles on the all-weather road going north. Unless he has a bicycle, the rest of the journey, another two miles along a narrow dirt road, must be completed on foot. During the July-August monsoon rains, this road is quickly transformed into a mud field and is closed to any but the most adven-turous pedestrian.

The houses in Manupur are huddled together in the center of the village. Those occupied by the "high" castes

---

*A *tempoo* is an auto-taxi. It resembles a medium-sized station-wagon, open at the back. Its normal safe capacity is six passengers. A *tempoo* from Khanna, however, usually carries anywhere from twelve to fourteen passengers. The discomfort and danger of the ride is compensated for by a lower price.

are usually two stories high, and are more and more frequently built with sun-dried or oven-baked bricks. They line the narrow streets paved with cobblestones, paid for by the village *Panchayat.** The "low" castes live in low mud houses along streets that are merely well-worn stretches of earth, liberally punctuated with puddles in the rainy season. The village center is surrounded by the fields where the majority of the village population works. Manupur is thus two large concentric circles: the inner for habitation, the outer for cultivation.

Table 2 gives a breakdown of the population of Manupur along caste lines. It also lists the traditional occupations, although they may not necessarily be followed in contemporary Manupur. The seasonal migrant labor that comes from Uttar Pradesh (north of Delhi), mostly single and transient, is excluded from these figures.

The Farmers

It is the Jats who have traditionally been the cultivators of the land. They represent nearly 60 percent of the total population, and by and large remain today in their traditional occupation. Furthermore, all of the cultivators but one in Manupur are Jats. Table 3 shows their breakdown by occupation.

As can be seen, almost 95 percent of occupied Jats are farmers; we shall thus use the term to mean owner-cultivator.

As stated before, our purpose here is to understand the material conditions of the farmer's existence, and to specify what influence these have on the size of his family.

---

*The *Panchayat* is the elected five-person village council.

Table 2

Population and Caste in Manupur*

Caste	Traditional Occupation
Agricultural:	
Jats ("high" landowning caste)	Farmers
Achutas ("outcastes")	
Chamar	Leather workers
Majbi	Sweepers
Julaha	Weavers
Service:	
Traditionally "high" service castes	
Brahmin	Priest, traditional doctor, moneylender, etc.
Khatri, Sonar	Shopkeeper, goldsmith
Traditionally "low" service castes	
Lohar-Tarkhan	Blacksmith-carpenter
Nai	Barber
Marasi	Drum beater
Gujjar	Herdsman
Kashmiri	Corder
Jheevar	Water carrier
Darzi	Tailor
Ghumar	Potter, builder

*This table is a result of a census I took in Manupur in the summer of 1970. In the case of the Jats, only 134 (88.2 percent) of the 152 families were contacted. These 134 families account for 990 Jats.

Table 2—Continued

Number and percent population	Total numbers	Total percentages
	1122	59.5
	445	23.6
(218—11.6%)		
(45—2.4%)		
(182—9.6%)		
	101	5.4
(81—4.3%)		
(20—1.1%)		
	218	11.6
(90—4.8%)		
(13—0.7%)		
(16—0.8%)		
(1—0.1%)		
(1—0.1%)		
(53—2.8%)		
(30—1.6%)		
(14—0.7%)		
Totals	1886	100.1

To compute the total Jat population of Manupur, I have used the 88.2 percent sample as being representative of the total Jat population. There seems to be no reason to believe that this was not the case.

This is not to say the Khanna Study totally ignored the farmer's material interests, or their influence on his behavior. From the outset, the directors of the study reasoned that the farmer would be interested in limiting his children because of his fear of the fragmentation of land: since inherited land holdings had been becoming increasingly smaller in size, it was thought that the farmer would

Table 3
Jats and their Occupations

Sector of the economy	Occupation	Numbers	%
Agricultural	Farmers	260	
	Farm laborer	1	
		261	94.9
Commerce and Industry	Taxi owner-drivers	2	
	Flour mill owner-operators	3	
		5	1.8
Skilled Services	Teachers	6	
	Cooperative Society secretaries	2	
		8	2.9
Unskilled Services	School janitor	1	0.4
		275	100.0
Unemployed	Educated*	3	
	Others	—	
Noneconomic activity	Priest	1	
	Retired or disabled	25	
	College students	8	
		37	

*By "educated" are meant those who have completed high school and have at least some college education. "Others" refers to those who have not had any formal education beyond the high school level.

be interested in at least slowing down this process by planning a smaller family. Furthermore, whereas in the past only male children inherited land, the situation had been radically altered by the passage of the Hindu Code Bill in 1956. This bill, by conferring equal rights of inheritance on children of both sexes, had further accelerated the pace of fragmentation.

The general problem of fragmentation comprises two specific and distinct problems. The first arises from the division of the farmer's total land holding when his children inherit his property. The second arises from the fact that farmers in Manupur *begin* with physically fragmented pieces. For example, when a farmer owns twelve acres, they are almost never contiguous. A twelve-acre holding may be split into three separate holdings of six, four, and two acres, three plots at varying distances from the village and usually characterized by varying degrees of productivity. When the twelve acres are divided up among four children, all three separate pieces will be divided into four equal shares and distributed to each heir. An heir will receive three acres, but as three different pieces of land: one of 1.5 acres, one of 1 acre, and one of 0.5 acre. There is only one rationale behind such a practice: to be fair.* Since each fragment differs in productivity and thus in value, it is deemed fair that the heirs get an equal share of every piece of land.

This problem has been successfully dealt with a number of times by the Punjab government. Land consolidation is undertaken at periodic intervals—at various times in the 1960s for the villages in the Khanna Study area—to

---

*It is also true that having scattered holdings in fragmented pieces, all varying in productivity, can be a form of insurance against the uncertainty of natural conditions.

give each farmer one continuous large piece of land roughly amounting in size to the two or three smaller pieces. Government-directed consolidation of land does not, however, solve the problem of the division of land through inheritance. A son might own a single plot, but he still owns much less than his father did, for the rest of the land was inherited by his brothers or sisters.

So the Khanna Study was quite right in maintaining that a major problem confronting the farmer in Punjab in general and in Manupur in particular was that of the fragmentation of land. It was, however, one major problem, and neither the only nor the primary problem facing the farmer. When both the individual family unit and the contemporary generation are considered, another dimension is added to the picture which diminishes the significance of land fragmentation.

Although the joint family in Manupur is increasingly breaking up, it is still true that a Jat family will stay together as an economic unit at least as long as the father lives. Sons do not leave their father's household because the only material basis for an agricultural life is the possession of land, and that becomes possible when the son inherits from the father.* Thus the farmer can realistically expect whatever land he inherits and whatever he manages to buy to remain intact during his lifetime. The problem of the fragmentation of land is the problem of the next generation, of tomorrow. The farmer's major problem is to make a living off the land in his own lifetime, to meet the costs of production in the present generation. The problem of production costs is the problem of today.

In order to appreciate the material conditions affecting

---

*The only exception to this is the well-educated son who gets a job outside Manupur or leaves to join the military or the police.

the Jats in Manupur, it is necessary to understand that although the Jats are the dominant caste, there exists a significant differentiation within the group. The differentiation results from different amounts of land owned by the various Jat families. On examination, three different groups emerge: those with small holdings (zero to five acres), those with medium holdings (six to sixteen acres), and those with large holdings (seventeen acres or more). The significance of the land fragmentation and of production costs is different for each of these three groups; the

Table 4
*Ownership of Land Among Jat Families in Manupur**

Nature of holding	Size of holding (acres)	Farmer families Numbers	%	Average land holding (acres)	% of village land held
Small	0-5	49	37.4	3.7	14.8
Medium	6-16	68	51.9	10.0	55.5
Large	17 or more	14	10.7	26.1	29.7
Total		131	100.0		100.0

*The statistics in Table 4 are from information obtained from the 131 land-owning Jat families interviewed. The figures can nevertheless be assumed to be characteristic of the entire Jat community (see note to Table 2). Detailed land records going back for decades were obtained from the village *Patwari* (accountant) and compared with the information from the individual families. It was found that the Patwari records were faulty in one respect: they gave an impression of land holdings being smaller than they actually are because prosperous farmers, aware of the possibility of land reform, listed part of their holdings under the name of a relative or a family member, while listing another part under their own names. This is why I have chosen to disregard the Patwari records and use the information obtained from the individual families.

problem of fragmentation increases in significance as one moves from small to large holdings, while the opposite is true when production costs are considered.

The farmers with small holdings are the living victims of the process of land fragmentation. They stand only a few steps away from material ruin. The land they hold is *already* small; their total concern is with making ends meet in the present, with reducing their costs of production as much as possible. Given a very small income, to have to hire even one farm hand can mean disaster. If such a farmer is merely to survive, he must rely on his family for the necessary labor power. If he is to think of any advancement, which every farmer in such a precarious position does, he must add to his family labor force and thus augment his resources. Every farmer interviewed in this group expressed the hope that with a large enough family—especially with one spaced close together—a few children could be spared to live away from the family land, thus accumulating some savings and perhaps buying more land, land which could be worked with the manpower available within the family itself.

This hope is not totally in vain; it is, in fact, based on the knowledge that a number of such precedents exist in the village. One such case is Mihan Singh. Mihan Singh's father once owned twelve acres of land. Since he was alone and his sons were too young to work the farm, farming twelve acres would have meant incurring too many costs. So he sold some of his land and took on odd jobs to support the family. By the time he died, eight of the twelve acres had been sold. Mihan Singh and his five brothers were left with four acres. The family decided to stay together, since splitting up the land would have meant individually acquiring uneconomic plots. The six brothers farmed the four acres and rented as many more acres as they could from others.* From their earnings they bought more land. Gradually, over the years, the size of their holding increased to twenty-five acres.

Per acre of land, it is the farmers with the least land who need the most labor. They are the ones least likely to have either a tubewell or a mechanical chaffcutter. As another farmer, talking of Mihan Singh and his brothers, said: "Why pay 2500 rupees for an extra hand? Why not have a son? . . . Instead of land fragmentation, more sons increase your land." This feeling prevails among most farmers in Manupur—in fact, among all but those who have large holdings. Although the farmers with medium holdings are concerned about their sons inheriting small pieces of land and joining the ranks of the poor, they maintain that the only way out is to have enough sons who can themselves work and buy more land. For while it is true that, as a result of recent changes in agricultural technology, farming has become increasingly productive, and that the incomes of farmers have increased in proportion to both the increase in agricultural production and in the prices for agricultural produce, there has also been a corresponding increase in the cost of production in the same period. The machines were paid for by taking loans from the Cooperative Society, and these must be repaid. The operation and repair of machinery costs money. And a rise in labor costs has accompanied the intensification of agriculture.† Even with a tubewell and a mechanical chaffcutter, labor needs are relatively high. Without a

---

*There is a system of renting land in Manupur known as *Batai.* A farmer rents land from another for a year, pays all the production costs for that year, and at harvest time shares the crop with the owner on a fifty-fifty basis.

†This refers to a rise in money wages. For information concerning the rise in real wages, see pp. 90-91.

tractor, the mechanization of agriculture can only be considered marginal. These farmers must choose between the lesser of two evils: land fragmentation or higher productions costs. Discussing his dilemma, one Jat told me:

> I have no machinery.* Of course, I am worried about the fragmentation of land. But even before I worry about my land being divided up tomorrow, I must worry about making a living on it today. Just look around: no one without sons or brothers to help him farms his land. He rents it out to others with large families. Without sons, there is no living off the land. The more sons you have, the less labor you need to hire and the more savings you can have. If I have enough, maybe we will buy some more land, and then fragmentation will not matter.

There are eighteen Jats in Manupur who have rented out either all or most of their land; none has more than one grown-up son. One of these eighteen is Darbara Singh. He has eight acres of land and four children: two girls, aged fifteen and thirteen, and two boys, aged eight and six. His wife is dead. He has leased out all his land on a fifty-fifty basis. He explains:

> I don't have any manpower. No sons old enough to help me on the land. I can't do it alone. It's more profitable to lease out the land than to hire a few extra hands. When my sons are old enough, I shall get my land back and we'll till it together.

Darbara Singh is, in fact, following a familiar practice in Manupur. After all, Jagger Singh did the same and says he "is a happy man today." In 1940, Jagger Singh owned four acres. He was single and had few resources. Because

---

*Meaning no tractor; in Manupur, a tractor is a machine, a tube-well is not.

of his poverty, marriage was out of question, for no farmer would consent to give his daughter to a poor man.* Farming under such conditions was hardly an economic proposition, but instead of selling his land, Jagger Singh decided to lease it on a yearly basis. He put the income aside for a future time when he could get married, have a number of sons, get his land back and become a farmer "as I was meant to be." In the meantime, he decided to emigrate to Lailpur where he took up a job as a servant. For five years he worked and saved. In 1947, he returned to Manupur with his savings and found a wife from the neighboring village. Two sons and a daughter were born to his wife. Unfortunately, she could bear him no more children after that. Once again, he left his wife and children in Manupur and went out to work as a tractor driver. Finally, in 1958, Jagger Singh returned to Manupur. He had accumulated savings from the payments on the lease of his land. His sons had meanwhile worked for other farmers, collecting grass and tending animals, earning their meals and clothing. Now they were seventeen and fifteen years old. Jagger Singh got his land back at the end of the year. With his savings he bought agricultural implements and a pair of fine oxen. He also got a part-time job as janitor at the village secondary school. Today, during the sowing, weeding, and the harvesting seasons, he helps his sons early in the morning, in the afternoons, and in the evenings. By the summer of 1966, he and his two sons were farming not only the four acres they owned initially, but also two additional acres they had been able to lease from

---

*Because of a high death rate among females, there exists a strikingly high proportion of males in the Khanna Study area. As a result, "almost a fifth of men over age 25 remained unmarried; no women were available for them to marry" (see *The Khanna Study*, p. 202). The unmarried are, by and large, from among the poor.

others. Jagger Singh curses fate for not having bestowed more sons upon him, for then they could have leased more land. Already, he explains, he and his sons "work like donkeys."

Land is expensive in Manupur. In the summer of 1970, the cheapest land in the village was around 3,500 rupees an acre. As the Khanna Study had reported in 1969, "top quality land in ideal locations brought around 20,000 rupees per acre!" The study had reported land prices in 1960 at around 1,000 rupees an acre.[1] The market in land gets livelier every year. From the summer of 1969 to that of 1970, four farmers sold their land and went to Uttar Pradesh, where land is cheap, around 800 rupees an acre. Jagger Singh and many other farmers in his position find this a tempting proposition, to sell their land in Manupur at the prevailing price and migrate to Uttar Pradesh where they can have at least twice as much land. What keeps them from moving is not "population pressure"—quite the contrary. To migrate and farm elsewhere, a farmer needs monetary savings and a large enough labor force—that is, a large enough family—to guarantee self-sufficiency. But this is what Jagger Singh does not have. As he puts it: "In farming, there is no money if you don't have sons to help you."

There is a second reason why poor farmers in Manupur look upon emigration as a desirable alternative. The last decade has seen the accentuation of existing inequalities in land ownership. At the top, one can already see the emergence of a rural bourgeoisie. The most marked difference is found between this stratum and the rest of the land-owning peasantry. In the middle stratum, more and more peasants find themselves pushed into the ranks of the small holders, while a number of small holders are left with meager, uneconomic holdings. If it were possible, they would prefer that their sons leave farming and join the ranks of the urban or rural proletariat. What prevents them from doing this are the taboos of the caste system: the system that once ensured their separation from Achuta farm labor has now turned upon them, and their resentment against caste obligations is easily discernible. Their numbers, however, are few, and caste still serves the interests of the dominant in Manupur. Those who have large families and some savings attempt to sell their land and move out of Manupur. The rest remain bitter and desperate, set against tradition, against caste, and open to a radical alternative.

The case of Gurdev Singh reflects the problems a farmer with medium-sized holdings must contend with in Manupur—the more so because Gurdev Singh is considered a "prosperous" farmer.

When Gurdev Singh retired from the military in 1966, he came back to Manupur eager to re-establish himself as a farmer. He took possession of the 5.5 acres he had rented out at the beginning of every year he spent in the army. To this 5.5 acres he added another 5.5 acres he bought. The money for this came from his savings, accumulated while he was in the service, and from the rent received on his land. It amounted to 10,000 rupees. Besides that, now that he was fifty-five years old and retired, he was entitled to a military pension, a monthly sum of 250 rupees, replenishing his finances to the tune of 3,000 rupees a year.

Captain Gurdev Singh is a most atypical Jat in Manupur. He owns eleven acres of land. He is also a retired military captain with a yearly pension of 3,000 rupees; only seventeen farmers in Manupur receive any pension from the military. Because of these two assets, Gurdev Singh was able to buy a tubewell and a mechanical chaff-cutter, and was able to electrify both without having to take a loan from the Cooperative Society. It is clear that a financial problem for Gurdev Singh will be magnified for those whose monetary assets are less sizable, that is, for nearly 75 percent of the farmers in Manupur.

Gurdev Singh's total yearly earnings can be itemized as follows:

Income for 1969-70
(in rupees)

Agricultural income	
Wheat crop	8,625
Corn	1,250
Cotton	665
Groundnuts (peanuts)	660
Oilseeds	500
	11,700
Military pension	3,000
	14,700

Gurdev Singh has some liabilities, however. His wife is a case of secondary sterility.* His one daughter is married, and his second son (nineteen years old) is in the military.† His eldest son (twenty-one years old) farms alongside him. Obviously, two men cannot work eleven acres, so Gurdev Singh must hire one sharecropper for the entire year, two laborers for a month each during the sowing seasons, four men for ten days during weed-

---

*"Secondary sterility" means that a woman has become sterile after bearing a certain number of children.

†The military, because of the steady and sizable pension after service, has great attractions for the village people. But since few can afford to have a son leave the family enterprise, not many are able to go into the military.

I. *Production costs*

    A. Equipment and operating costs

Chemical fertilizers	2,200 rupees
Electricity and oil for tubewell*	700
Motor repair	300
Grain, salt, linseed oil for two	
buffaloes and pair of oxen	1,000
Bicycle repair	50
Oxcart repair	450
Land tax	55
Rifle and bicycle license	23
	4,778

    B. Labor Costs

Wages	3,585
Food†	660
	4,245

II. *Household maintenance costs*

Food	2,640
Clothing	500
Radio license	15
Medical expenses	175
Electricity for the house	60
	3,390
Total expenditure	12,413

Gurdev Singh's Family Budget

Total income	14,700
Total expenditure	12,413
Savings	2,287

---

*Electrical supply is often switched off in the rural sections of the Punjab, forcing the farmer to switch the operation of his tubewell to oil, which is more expensive.

†A laborer must be fed all meals for the day he works for the farmer. This includes breakfast, lunch, dinner, and mid-morning, afternoon, and night tea.

ing time, five men for two weeks during the wheat harvest, and one man for five days during the maize harvest. All together, this amounts to hiring 540 days of labor.

Gurdev Singh also grows enough lentils, onions, eggplants, tomatoes, ginger, and peppers for his family's consumption. He also sets aside a piece of land for planting grass for the oxen, the buffalo, and the cows. Since this produce is consumed by his family, we exclude it from his family budget.

His costs can be computed under three separate headings: equipment and operating costs, labor costs, and household costs. The first two added together give us an idea of his production costs.

A number of observations may be made. What has been presented here is a minimal budget: * the expenses listed are all essential and could not be significantly decreased even if Gurdev Singh were replaced by another personality with a totally different set of inclinations, provided that the number of residents in the family were the same: father, mother, son, son's wife, and their daughter.

---

*This minimal budget excludes a number of secondary expenses. The most important is that of gifts. In Manupur, both the giving and receiving of gifts to and from one's kin on specific social and religious occasions is obligatory. This practice, while transcending village boundaries, exists strictly within caste lines. It thus serves to enhance caste solidarity. Secondly, entertainment expenses are also excluded. These are almost solely confined to the purchase of liquor. The brewing of liquor at home is illegal in Punjab, and infrequent raids are carried out by the town police on the villagers' homes to identify and arrest the culprits. Home brewing is still a common practice among most poor families. Gurdev Singh buys, on the average, four bottles of liquor a month for himself and his friends. As he says, hospitality costs money. The gesture is always reciprocated by his friends.

What is most important is the fact that had Gurdev Singh not been the recipient of a military pension, his total earnings—11,700 rupees—would have fallen short of his minimal expenses—12,413 rupees. This would have been the case because of his inordinately high labor costs, 4,245 rupees. His only alternative would have been to lease at least part of his land. As he explained, if he had more sons, his labor costs would be significantly reduced and his household maintenance costs only marginally increased. Labor costs are the only variable part of a farmer's production costs, and they can be significantly lowered only by having a large family. Every farmer knows that the cost of having each child declines the more children he has. The benefits, on the other hand, increase. Gurdev Singh expressed the hope that his second son would soon be married and that his two daughters-in-law would bear him many grandsons so that in the near future they could accumulate enough savings to buy more land. A saying among the Jats goes:

A forest is not made of one tree
A Jat is not made of one son.

Prosperous farmers, those with seventeen or more acres of land, number fourteen (10.7 percent) in Manupur. It is at this level that the land fragmentation–production cost dilemma is successfully resolved. The average amount of land owned by families in this category is 26.3 acres. Only such a family has the necessary land, revenue, and the repayment capacity to take a large enough loan from the state-owned Land Mortgage Bank to buy a tractor and embark on the road to full mechanization. Of the prosperous farmers, 35.7 percent (5 out of the 14) own tractors,* whereas a mere 2.6 percent (3 out of 117) of the rest of the farmers own a tractor. (Significantly, two of these three have an outside source of income—a son working in the city—and one has only part-time use of his tractor since he loans it out to two other farmers.)

The immediate result of full mechanization is to reduce the labor requirement drastically and to simultaneously increase productivity. For example, with a tractor and all the necessary implements, it takes three people—a cultivator, his son, and a farm laborer—to work fifty acres of land. Without a tractor, the same land requires at least fourteen people year round, and at least twenty at sowing, weeding, and harvesting time.

It would be a mistake, however, to suppose that families with tractors are necessarily any smaller than other families in Manupur. Although a farmer whose need for labor has been significantly reduced through mechanization attaches much more importance to the future fragmentation of his land and its effects on the prosperity of his sons, he still has a number of children. This is for two reasons: he lives in an environment where a large family is generally considered an asset, a society that looks favorably on having many children;† and, more importantly, mechanization has taken place only in this generation, so its effect on limiting the family will not be discernible at

---

*The smallest tractor—a Russian-made DT-14, using fourteen horsepower—costs 9,000 rupees at the official list price. But it is only available in the black market, where the price is 13,000 rupees. During the summer of 1970, even the black market could not supply this tractor. Thus a farmer in Manupur had to settle for a larger, second-hand tractor (thirty-seven horsepower) and pay 25,000 rupees for it in the black market. A number of prosperous farmers would like to buy a tractor but are confronted by this dilemma.

†The social environment will be discussed in detail in Chapter 6.

least until the next generation. It is therefore true that the newly married sons of the mechanized farmers are the Jat group most favorable to the idea of family planning through the use of modern contraception.

There is one major obstacle to the spread of total mechanization in Manupur to others besides the prosperous farmer. Along with problems regarding the availability of capital, and of the tractor itself, other farmers are caught in a major dilemma, one from which there is no escape without structural change: the ownership of a tractor cannot be an economic proposition unless the farmer has a sizable holding—according to the farmers themselves, at least fifteen acres—and this rules out over 85 percent of the farmers in Manupur. If agriculture is to be further mechanized, productivity increased, and the small family made a "rational" choice, then the pattern of ownership of land in Manupur must change. The prerequisite for technological change is no less than a change in the social structure.

The Farm Laborers

In traditional Manupur, the caste system alone determined the allocation of labor in the village: the caste a child was born into specified the work he would do as an adult. The exchange of goods and services was conducted through a customary barter system, and here caste operated in the form of the *Jajmani* system, which spelled out the relations between the *Jajman*—the employer, of "high" caste—and those who worked for them, the *Kamin*—the clients, of "low" caste.*

---

*The Jajman came from the dominant caste, which owned the best land in each village, while the Kamin came from both the nonculti-

Under the Jajmani system, the *Majbi* (sweeper) cleaned the house of his Jajman, took away the dead animals (those under six months of age), and collected the animal dung to be used either as fertilizer or fuel. When the farmer needed extra hands, as during harvest time, the Majbi also worked in the fields. The *Chamar* (leather worker) was a *Sanji*, a year-round agricultural laborer, paid in kind, and took care of the farmer's animals and disposed of the dead ones (those above six months of age). His family ate the meat off the corpses, and he made leather from the skins and sold it to the merchant in Khanna. Both the Chamar and the Majbi were available for any menial work their Jajman needed done. They were the lowest of the low, the Achutas, the outcaste "untouchables." During the harvest season, they assisted in harvesting and in return received a bundle of grain at the end of the day. The payment aimed at assuring a bare subsistence and had little relation to the work performed.

The material position of the Achutas was related to a corresponding subservient social position. They were the

---

vating service castes (such as the barber, the blacksmith, the priest) and the cultivating but landless castes (the Achutas, or "untouchables"). The barber, the blacksmith, and the priest provided those necessary services for the land-owning "high" caste—or castes, as the case may be, depending on the village concerned. All over India, although the Brahmins theoretically occupied the apex of the caste pyramid, they were in social ascendance only when they effectively controlled the best lands in the village. When this was not the case, the Brahmins were typically priests in the service of the land-owning or commercial castes, whichever were dominant, conferring ritual prestige upon them. Without material power to back it up, the caste status of the Brahmin had little social relevance. Thus the case of Manupur, where, before British colonialism created the social conditions that led to the dominance of the Brahmin moneylenders, the Brahmins were maintained by the land-owning "high" caste Jats.

"unlucky" ones. Touching them, and at certain times even seeing them, was something to be avoided. If a member of a "high" caste was polluted by their touch, he had to undergo repeated ritual washing. Their housing area was both segregated and situated according to caste taboos.*

The Jajmani system functioned best in a society where labor was abundant and cheap, the level of technology low, the economy relatively unchanging, and social mobility practically nonexistent. There the Achutas had no choice but to work for the upper castes for small rewards: daily meals and two sets of clothing a year. The decline of the Brahmin aristocracy and the introduction of numerous technological changes in agriculture have significantly altered the demand for farm labor and served to undermine the Jajmani system.

The relationship between the mechanization of agriculture and the need for labor is a changing one, and needs to be understood for the various stages of mechanization. While the operation of the Persian wheel required both human and animal labor, the tubewell only needs supervision from one individual, and that for a short period of time. The introduction of the mechanical chaffcutter has also had the effect of eliminating the demand for one kind of labor. Other effects of the new agricultural technology, however, have more than offset this decline. The tubewell has made possible rapid and planned irrigation, a prerequisite to intensive, "scientific" agriculture; the introduction of chemical fertilizers and Kalyan wheat has done

---

*As one Jat explained to me, the wind in Manupur blows most often from east to west, sometimes from north to south, and least of all from west to east. Therefore, the Achutas live on the western side of most Punjab villages since that would minimize the possibility of their polluting the air before it gets to the higher castes.

the same. Partial mechanization has thus intensified agricultural production, raised yields, and increased the work load. The process has been further accentuated by the added acreage devoted to wheat. The cumulative effect of partial mechanization has been a marked rise in the demand for farm labor—although this increase is, for the most part, seasonal, that is, for the half-year devoted to weeding, sowing, and harvesting.

Total mechanization—specifically, the introduction of the tractor—has begun to reverse this process, but since tractor ownership remains limited to eight (2 percent) of the cultivators, its effect is marginal.

Overall, then, the result of the technology introduced since the 1950s has been to increase the demand for farm labor. This rising demand has been accompanied by a change both in hiring practices and in wage structure. Because of the increased agricultural yield, government support of higher grain prices, and the highly uneven demand for labor during the year, farmers now prefer to hire daily wage labor, or even yearly wage labor, rather than promise a share of the crops. The laborers, on the other hand, given the rising yields *and* the higher crop prices, would rather be paid in kind, a share of the crop they reap to harvest.

The daily money wage has doubled in the last decade, from 2.50 rupees in 1960 to 4.00-6.00 rupees in 1970; different wages are paid at sowing, weeding, and harvesting times. Yearly wages are usually around 1,500 rupees. All laborers, whether crop-sharers or wage laborers, are provided with all of the day's meals. Prices, however, have also increased. As the Khanna Study reported, wheat and sugar prices have "more than doubled" from 1960 to 1969. Wheat, it should be remembered, is both the major crop and the major part of the diet in Manupur. The price of maize, cotton, and peanuts "also increased, though in lesser degree."[2] This means that real wages from 1960 to 1970 probably remained constant, or if there was an increase, it was only minimal. The crucial change in the position of the Sanji, as that of most labor in Manupur, has been that whereas in the past the Sanji received a customarily specified payment, regardless of the amount of work he did, today the payment the Sanji receives in Manupur bears a definite relation to the work he does (i.e., he receives not two bundles of wheat at the end of the day, but a certain percentage of the harvest). In short, labor is becoming a commodity in Manupur. Feudal relations of work are giving way to capitalist relations of work.

Despite the farmers' growing preference for wage labor, the seasonal shortage of labor in Manupur and the surrounding area has strengthened the bargaining power of the laborers and kept the wage-labor system from becoming universal. But since even in crop-sharing the reward is directly related to the effort expended in a given amount of time, the farmers prefer seasonal crop-sharing: an entire family will contract to harvest a piece of land from the cultivator, who will pay them a share—usually 1/25 of the total harvest—as a reward. Finally, in those cases where the Sanji is still employed, the farmer will subtract the proportional cost of chemical fertilizers from his yearly share of the produce. Depending upon the number of Sanjis employed, a share will range anywhere from 1/10 to 1/16 of the annual crop.

One effect of these changes has been that the influence of the Jajmani system has been drastically diminished. Not only have the numbers of those who work under the system been reduced, but the claim the system has on their labor time has also been significantly curtailed. Traditionally, the Jajmani system prescribed the use of all of the labor time of all the "low" caste members in the village. Today only about 30 percent of the Achutas in Manupur have Jajmans. Furthermore, the time given to the Jajmans is now only three days a year.*

Although there has been some improvement in their material and legal position, and although neither the Chamar nor the Majbi is today necessarily confined to his traditional caste occupation, the *Harijans* (the new name for the "untouchables")† still belong to the lowest class. As Table 5 indicates, agriculture forms the core of the Chamars' occupation today.

The Majbis (sweepers) have also begun to leave their traditional occupation—picking up animal dung to make organic fertilizers and fuel—and have started to join the agricultural labor force. Although all the farmers in Manupur use chemical fertilizers, an overwhelming majority

---

*Both the work and its rewards are now specified. On one day, the Kamin will dispose of any dead animal for the Jat, or repair any damage done to his property by heavy rains. If his services are required for another day during the year, the farmer will have to pay him. The remaining two days are marked for agricultural labor: one for weeding during the wheat crop, the other for the same during the maize or corn crop. The returns for this labor are twenty kilos of wheat and twenty kilos of corn or maize. A small gift is also given by the Jajman at wedding and engagement ceremonies and at the birth of a son. The "gift" is always two rupees.

†Previously known as *Achutas* (the "untouchables"), today the Chamars and Majbis are called *Harijans* (the "children of God"), a term introduced by Mahatma Gandhi and sanctified by the force of law, and a term almost universally resented by the Achutas for the paternalism it connotes. A number of legal changes have also formally affected the position of the Chamars and the Majbis. The law specifies that one of the five members of the village Panchayat be an Achuta. In Manupur, the other members are always Jats, and the Panchayat is, in effect, a watchdog over the interests of the farmers.

Table 5
Chamars and their Occupations*

Sector of the economy	Occupation	Total	%
Agriculture	Cultivators	2	
	Sanji, or yearly wage labor	50	
	Daily wage labor	24	
	Herding and trading of animals	14	
	Sons tending animals	13	
		103	92.0
Commerce	Shopkeepers	2	1.8
Skilled services	Teacher	1	0.9
Unskilled services	Nonagriculture labor	4	
	House servant	1	
	Watchman (for the school)	1	
		6	5.3
	Total	112	100.0

*This listing of Chamars actually lists both the Chamar and the Julaha castes (traditionally leather workers and weavers, respectively). Even before the recent changes in the village, the Julaha did the same work as the Chamars, and today there exists no difference between the work of the two. The following additional points should also be noted:

Traditionally, the word Sanji was used for a yearly agricultural laborer who was paid in kind. Today it is also used for a yearly wage laborer, which is what most Sanji are now.

The category "skilled services" excludes clerks (two), mechanics (two), and welfare worker (one), who have moved out of the village, though their parents and families remain.

The subcategory "nonagricultural laborer" excludes one nonagricultural laborer who works and lives outside the village, though his family resides in Manupur. Of the four listed, three (two electrical workers) live in the village but commute to work in Khanna. The fourth works in the flour mill in Manupur.

still use organic fertilizers as a supplement, but leave it
to their children to collect the dung every morning, pre-
ferring to hire the Majbis for other tasks.

Table 6
Majbis and their Occupations

Sector of the economy	Occupation	Total	%
Agriculture	Making dung cakes	14	66.7
	Sanji, or yearly wage labor	6	28.6
	Son tending to animals	1	4.8
		21	100.1
Noneconomic activity	Retired and disabled (military pensioner)	1	

Once we realize that the Achutas comprise the core of
the agricultural labor force in Manupur today, it is easier
to understand why social change has reinforced the value
of the large family among agricultural laborers. First,
crop-sharing—when an entire family contracts to harvest
a piece of land—has led to a radical change in the composition of the labor force and in the attitudes toward girl
children. Women and girls now work side by side with
their husbands and brothers: the more hands a family can
muster, the more land it can contract from the cultivator.
The inclusion of women in the agricultural labor force
means that "low" caste families do not look upon the birth
of a girl baby with as much disfavor as used to be the case.
Obviously, the disfavor still persists to a degree, since the
daughter will marry and emigrate precisely when she has
reached the age of greatest productivity.

The second factor enhancing the attraction of the large
family is the creation and proliferation of wage labor.
Even where a laborer is paid in kind, the payment he

receives bears a definite relation to the work he does. The Achuta is no longer tied to his Jajman for life, performing multiple tasks for a subsistence living; today he is a farm laborer who pledges his employer a certain period of services for specified wages. But this means that he is subject to the periods of employment and layoff of the labor market. The seasonality of employment becomes much more obvious and important since it is related to the income of the laborer. Work is most intensive during the harvest, weeding, and sowing seasons, and it remains, as it has always been, labor-intensive. Thus, although there is a shortage of labor in Manupur, it exists only during specific seasons, for a little over half a year. During the other half, there is considerable unemployment. Overall, farm labor in Manupur is underemployed.

But this does not mean that the farm laborer is not interested in increasing his family labor force. Quite the contrary. No matter how large his family, as long as agricultural production is characterized by low technology, there will always be a clear demarcation between those times of the year when labor is in great demand and those times when it is not; his income will depend upon the amount of work his family can contract during the busy season. A larger family means a greater income during the busy season and higher savings for the slow season.

Seasonality of employment has one other effect. During periods of low employment, farm laborers turn to the market town of Khanna and seek temporary employment there. Only a few succeed since the labor market in Khanna is a year-round market and has few temporary jobs. This leads a number—very few today (only four, less than 5 percent), and yet a growing trend—to leave the agricultural economy altogether and seek *yearly* wage labor in Khanna. The problem is that there is not even the seasonal job security there is in Manupur; the laborer is subject to the whims of his employer. It is only those from large families, who have resources to fall back on, who hazard such a move.

For one who labors in the field, the day centers around work. Time for relaxation or for tending to personal needs is usually found between different types of work. This is true for both the farmer and the farm laborer: they labor together in the same field, and are usually involved in the same activity. The only time they work separately is in the early hours of the dawn and late in the evening when both tend to their own cattle. They cannot be distinguished by the clothes they wear during work hours, and both eat what the farmer's wife cooks them.

The day begins early for a farmer in Manupur, around four in the morning. He must first feed the animals (oxen, cows, buffalo) and give them water. While the oxen contentedly chew the grass, the farmer hurries through his daily preliminaries. These include going to the fields to relieve himself, breaking a twig off the Datan tree to brush his teeth, and drinking a cup of tea.

The oxen are tied to the cart at around five o'clock in the morning and the men are ready to go to the fields and work. Work lasts until seven in the evening, interrupted only for "fueling oneself" (as the farmers are fond of saying)—that is, for breakfast in mid-morning (15 minutes around 10:00), lunch (from 12:00 to 1:00), and tea (from 4:00 to 4:15). If it is a hot summer day, lunch might last for two hours instead of one. Meals are brought to the field by the son, or, if necessary, by the daughter.* The

---

*This "necessity" results from the sexual division of labor in Manupur. A woman's task is said to be in the home, a man's outside. There

distance between the house and the farm is sometimes over a mile, and it would be a waste of precious time to go home.

When it begins to get dark—and in the summer this is usually around seven in the evening—oxen are reharnessed to the cart and everybody proceeds home. During sowing and harvest times, work may go on as late as 10:00 P.M. Once home, the animals must be tended. If the farmer has a young son, grass has already been cut; if not, he must employ someone to do it. It remains for him to prepare the fodder, and to feed, wash, and clean the animals.

His daily chores over around 8:45, the farmer washes and then has dinner at 9:00. His wife serves while he and the laborers eat. Food is usually wheat or corn cakes, depending on the time of the year, and one of the vegetables he grows in his fields. During the meal the radio plays popular music. A few times during the week everybody listens to a special radio program on the latest farming methods. If there is a good storyteller in the group—and the villagers complain the art is gradually being lost with the advent of the radio—there will be a little entertainment for the evening. There will be talk of the "bravery of the male" and the "deceit of the weaker sex," of the intrigues among kings and princes, and tales of "golden lands beyond the horizon"— a little dreaming before sleep overcomes weary bodies. By around ten the village is asleep.

The routine changes a little during the winter harvest,

---

is status associated with keeping women within the house. So a daughter will walk to the fields to deliver meals only if she has no brother, if he is too small, or if he is occupied—that is, only if necessary."

when the men often build grass huts in the field and spend the night there. Little sleep is possible, for that part of the field which has been harvested during the day must be watered at night.

The farmer's wife has an even greater burden of work. She must prepare the meals (breakfast, lunch, and dinner) and tea (early morning, mid-afternoon, and late night). Meals are made for the husband and the children and, if there are few children, for the laborers who have to be hired. The work is hard. Flour must be mixed with water and made into dough, and dough into wheat or corn cakes, usually six cakes per person per meal. The buffalo must be milked twice a day, morning and evening. The milk is used to make *lassi*, a yoghurt drink for warm mornings, and to make butter late in the evening. Dishes must be washed after every meal.

There is more. Animal dung must be collected and put in a pit to dry out. (The Majbis only collect dung from the fields, not from around the house.) She must build a dungcake fire, which provides a slow and gentle heat over which to simmer a lentil curry. While it is cooking, she attends to other tasks. Firewood must also be cut, gathered, and carried to the house. The buffalo must be given drinking water and fed grass if the husband is in the fields at night. Clothes must be washed every day. Cleaning a dirty piece of clothing—and there is a lot of dirt in the fields—means soaking it in soapy water and then beating it with a wooden stick. The use of simple tools requires both time and effort. Younger children have to be tended to, fed, and washed. In the midst of all this, the wife must somehow find time to feed herself.

The farm laborer's wife has very similar duties, with one important difference: she only has to cook for the young, the old, and the women in the household. The male members of the family, when at work, are fed by the farmer's wife.

The wealthiest farmers, five in Manupur, are an exception to this description. Their time is increasingly devoted to managerial functions, and less to labor in the fields: they are becoming landlords and are no longer farmers. In one case, the wife even has domestic help from an Achuta girl.

The farmer's children can be of considerable assistance, even while they are young. A son or daughter can bring grass and water for the cattle before going to school at eight in the morning, can help in the field in the afternoon if necessary, and can graze the cattle in the evening. In fact, primary responsibility for the cattle can be left to the children and the adult's load lightened a little.

If a farmer's wife has no young children, it would mean intolerable hardship. She would then have to walk to the fields to deliver two meals and one tea every day. The walk over and back, the wait while everybody eats—so the utensils can be taken back, washed, and cleaned for the next meal—can take as much as four hours. Since women are expected to have children, they do not even learn to ride bicycles!

While it is true that an agricultural family expresses definite preference for a male over a female child, it is also true that after one or two sons have been born, one or two female babies are usually welcome additions to the family labor force. The farmer knows the likelihood of the extended family breaking up when he dies. He also knows that for over six months a year he may have to hire at least three laborers and that he must see that they are fed. Many a serious quarrel has been reported between a husband and a wife when, unaided by a daughter or a daughter-in-law, she finds the burden of cooking for so many, as well as doing the rest of her chores, overwhelming. Even one daughter in the family will relieve the wife's burden, and when it is time for her to marry, it will also be time for the sons to marry and bring their wives into the house.

Among Achuta families who are part of the agricultural labor force, it is not only the older sons and daughters who play an important role in augmenting family income; younger children play a role too. Some are employed by the farmers, earning their daily meals and two sets of clothing a year. The seasonality of employment does not affect child labor since children are mostly employed looking after cattle or doing housework. Besides working for the farmer, children also tend cattle at home. In an Achuta family, the care of the lone buffalo is almost always the responsibility of a young child. Many Achuta families own cattle, especially those who are farm laborers.

Table 7
Ownership of Cattle Among Jats and Achutas

Caste	Total families	Families owning at least one head of cattle	%
Jats	143*	140	97.9
Achutas	61	54	88.5

Among those Majbi families that are not a part of the agricultural labor force but gather animal waste for manure, women and older children have long worked alongside the men, while the younger children take care of the youngest ones at home.

The use of machine technology, the increased contact

---

*88.2 percent of the sample; see footnote, Table 2.

with the commercial world, the introduction to the modern credit system (through the Cooperative Society), and the general identification of "scientific" agriculture with material prosperity has meant a growing realization among the farmers that literacy and a high school education are not only beneficial, but necessary. If one is to keep on enjoying the benefits of the "new way," one must learn to master its techniques. At least one son must be educated through high school. As one farmer explained to me: "We must give our children enough education so that Brahmins won't rob us as they used to. If our children don't have education, then we will revert to previous ways on the land."

Table 8
Jat Children and their Enrollment in School

Description	Primary School (Grades 1-5)			Secondary School (Grades 6-10)		
	Total of school age	Total in school	%	Total of school age	Total in school	%
Boys	90	78	86.7	67	42	62.7
Girls	69	58	84.1	55	16	29.1
Total	159	136	85.5	122	58	47.5

As can be seen from Table 8, education is considered far more important for the male than for the female child. And yet, as a result of counteracting pressures, a number of girls do go to secondary school. Although the girl child will grow up, get married, and leave the village for "her family" (people talk of daughters as if they do not belong to their parents, but are born and reared for "other families"), an educated son, it is said, wants an educated wife.

The more educated a girl, the less dowry demanded by her future in-laws. In addition, high school education for both boys and girls has a practical value. Besides the usual academic subjects, girls are taught to manage the family budget; boys learn the latest farming techniques. Finally, school only takes up six hours; the rest of the time is usually spent assisting the family with its daily work.

It is important to realize that the marriage age among Jat girls has risen, regardless of whether they attend high school or not. This is for two reasons. First, the intensification of agriculture has increased the work load, not only in the field, but also in the farmer's home. The longer the daughter stays unmarried, the more assistance she can lend her family. Secondly, during the years she spends at home, the grown-up daughter can earn her dowry by sewing, spinning, and weaving. The increased access to Khanna means that at least some of what she makes can be sold there for cash. The remaining mats she weaves and clothes she stitches form a part of her dowry.

Education is free for Achuta children; other children must pay. The school is run by the village Panchayat, and the state pays the tuition of all Achuta children in school. While in theory primary education is compulsory for all children, in practice this is hardly the case. Table 9 shows how few Achuta children attend school.

Despite the fact that work remains of primary importance and school of secondary, it can be seen that a number of Achuta boys are able to remain in school. For one thing, until a boy is fifteen or so, work and education are compatible. Tending to cattle is a part-time job which can be accomplished after school. And even if a boy is sent on to secondary school, he usually only continues until he is old enough to start working as a full-time farm laborer, that is, until his earning power can be fully real-

Table 9
Achuta Children and their Enrollment in School

Description	Primary School (Grades 1-5)			Secondary School (Grades 6-10)		
	Total of school age	Total in school	%	Total of school age	Total in school	%
Boys	31	15	48.4	30	15	50.0
Girls	33	7	21.2	26	—	0.0
Total	64	22	34.3	56	15	26.8

ized. Although there are fifteen Achuta boys in the secondary school, six of them are in grade 6, three in grade 7, three in grade 8, two in grade 9, and only one in grade 10.

It is clear from the table that among Achuta families no importance is put upon secondary education for girls. Despite this, the marriage age has tended to rise, primarily because the girls are now included in the agricultural labor force at harvest time. The longer a girl stays unmarried, the longer she will contribute to the family income.

Among the agricultural classes in Manupur, the IADP successfully accomplished its goal: undermining the Brahmin moneylenders and encouraging the growth of a Jat rural bourgeoisie; the Khanna Study, however, was a total failure. Unlike the IADP, the Khanna Study did not respond to any concrete need felt by these people.

We have seen that the agricultural classes live in a society with a low level of technology, where survival as well as competition is conducted primarily on the basis of numbers; labor is the most important factor. For them, family planning means voluntarily reducing the family labor force. This would mean courting economic disaster and would, therefore, be extremely irrational. Not until the level of technology used by the majority of the villagers in their work is significantly raised can the attitude toward family planning change. This would be true no matter what program was introduced, or what workers staffed it.

Notes

1. *The Khanna Study,* p. 305.
2. Ibid.

5

The "Population Problem" and the Traditional Service Sector

The "new" technology in Manupur primarily affected the agricultural sector, and the resulting prosperity has led to the introduction of other advanced technology among the cultivating households. Its effect on the noncultivating households, on the other hand, has been catastrophic. Life has changed abruptly and cruelly. The introduction of a single innovation—for instance, the sewing machine—has totally destroyed the material base of many families' existence. What has happened in Manupur reflects in part, and in microcosm, the history of technological change in advanced capitalist societies: those who pay the cost of change do not necessarily reap its benefits. The history of Manupur in the last two decades is in part the history of the struggle of those not involved in agriculture to maintain some continuity in their lives in the face of a new wind.

The nonagricultural service sector in Manupur includes the traditional upper class as well as many of those who were a part of the lower classes, the prosperous as well as the poor. Its response to technological change is of

particular interest to us because it provides an opportunity to test the major assumption of the "overpopulation" theorists, that people should associate their poverty
with their large numbers and thus seek to limit their numbers in the face of adversity. The crucial question is, would
such a response be rational?

The response of the nonagricultural castes has taken
two forms. Since the "new" society created little work that
would ensure a continued adequate living outside the
agricultural sector, the only alternative for the "high"
castes, if their traditional living standards were even to
be approximated, was to emigrate. The prerequisite was
substantial savings or skills. For the rest, there was little
choice: they had to continue performing the traditional
tasks, where that remained possible, or else they had to
adapt to the "new" society by adapting to the needs of the
dominant classes.

Traditionally, the service castes—the tailor, the barber,
etc.—were integrated into the social and economic life of
the village through the Jajmani system, as were the agricultural castes. The importance of the Jajmani relationship
to the service castes was that it stipulated an exchange of
services for a customary right to a proportion of the crop
harvested by the cultivating castes. The terms of this exchange, however, reflected the distribution of political
power in the village, for the exchange was in no way
equal; the dominant castes appropriated the bulk of the
total harvest.

Since the relationship of the service castes to their
"high" caste Jajman was hereditary, the system in traditional Manupur eliminated any form of competition within
caste boundaries. And since all the other castes, including

the "high" castes, were proscribed from doing the work of any of the "low" service castes, any competition between castes was ruled out. Thus a farmer or Brahmin's wife could not stitch her own clothes but had to use the services of the family tailor. The tailor was, in turn, obligated to render such a service whenever it was demanded and was prohibited from doing any other work besides stitching clothes.

On the face of it, the Jajmani system would seem to guarantee occupational security to every member of the village. In fact, it served to insure the continuation of a rigidly hierarchical social system which severely limited any form of vertical mobility within the society.

The Jajmani system was destroyed as a system of social relationships because it no longer benefited the dominant caste—the Jats. Today the farmer's wife stitches many of the family's clothes (she has a sewing machine), pumps her own water, and shampoos her own hair—despite the fact that there are still a substantial number of tailor, water carrier, and barber families in the village. And even for those service castes which remain in their traditional occupations, payment no longer comes as a customary share of the agricultural produce since both the value and the amount of this produce have markedly increased. Payment is now in cash and for specific services rendered. The market economy has come to Manupur.

Marasi and Jheevar: The "New" Agricultural Proletariat

These are two members of the traditional "low" castes in Manupur whose occupations have been rendered totally obsolete as a result of technological change. In all, there are fifty-three *Jheevar* (water carriers) and sixteen *Marasi* (drum beaters). The water carrier has lost his job to the water pump. The drum beater is no longer needed now that the *Gurudwaras* (Sikh houses of worship) have equipped themselves with loudspeakers.

A lack of material resources or marketable skills rules out emigration as a feasible alternative for these people. The logical decision would be to join the agricultural labor force, for it is here that the village economy gives the greatest rewards to its "low" castes. This, however, has not been possible. Their familiarity with agricultural work and their skills in the field are nonexistent. Of all the "low" castes in Manupur, they are the least suited for farm labor. And even if they desired to enter the agricultural economy, they could not: the Jats need them to perform those tasks —such as being messengers to other villages—that no one else in the village would agree to do. The work is menial, time-consuming, and degrading, but the Jats are the "masters." A member of a small, financially weak group such as the water carriers would be foolish to displease his Jat and incur his wrath. It could make his life in the village impossible and emigration his only alternative. Further, there exists no alliance among the water carriers and the drum beaters. They are weak not only in terms of economic standing, but also in terms of numbers (there are ten water carrier and four drum beater families). These castes therefore exist as appendages to the farmers.

Fortunately, the same situation does not apply to their offspring. A child can perform a variety of unskilled tasks, such as collecting manure for the farmer or tending his cattle. He can begin with light agricultural work at a tender age and learn through experience. The son can join the agricultural proletariat and bring a modicum of material reward and happiness to his parents. The families of these groups are therefore usually large.

Let us take a few examples. Fakir Singh is a traditional water carrier. After he lost his job, he remained as a messenger for those Jat families which used to be his Jajmans, barely earning a subsistence living. He has eleven children, ranging in age from twenty-five to four. He says he told the Khanna Study workers he was "using" the foam tablets. When government family-planning workers later contacted him, he agreed to have a vasectomy, but repeatedly failed to appear on the appointed day, giving a more or less convincing excuse when approached again. Fakir Singh maintains that every one of his sons is an asset. The youngest one—aged five or six—collects hay for the cattle; the older ones tend those same cattle. Between the ages of six and sixteen, they earn 150 to 200 rupees a year, plus all their meals and necessary clothing. Those sons over sixteen earn 2,000 rupees and meals every year. Fakir Singh smiles and adds: "To raise children may be difficult, but once they are older it is a sea of happiness."

Another water carrier is Thaman Singh. When I went to talk to him, he mistook me for a Khanna Study worker who had returned for the summer. He welcomed me inside his home, gave me a cup of tea (with milk and "market" sugar, as he proudly pointed out later), and said:

> You were trying to convince me in 1960 that I shouldn't have any more sons. Now, you see, I have six sons and two daughters and I sit at home in leisure. They are grown up and they bring me money. One even works outside the village as a laborer. You told me I was a poor man and couldn't support a large family. Now, you see, because of my large family, I am a rich man.

For a member of a "low" caste, Thaman Singh is prosperous. As he emphasized, "Time has proven me right."

It is no wonder that the poor in Manupur try to emulate him and others like him.

Ghumar: Large Family for Prosperity

Unlike the water carrier and the drum beater, only some of the tasks traditionally performed by the *Ghumar* have been rendered obsolete by technological change. His traditional occupation was that of a brickmaker, builder, and potter. His building skills are of little use today since he only knew how to build *Kacha* houses. A Kacha house is made of mud and sun-dried bricks, is very cheap to construct, and is thus within the means of a poor agricultural family; it is also very susceptible to disintegration during the heavy monsoon rains. The newly prosperous Jats have rebuilt their dwellings into weather-resistant *Packa* houses. Bricks for these are brought from outside the village, where they are produced relatively cheaply by large-scale manufacturers. As a result, the Ghumar has lost a major part of his work; today he is confined to making pots for the farmers.

Since he has ceased to build their houses, the Ghumar has found the Jats unwilling to give him the customary share of the agricultural produce. Today he has no Jajmans, and no one gives him a yearly payment. Whoever buys his pots pays him for each pot purchased, and payment has increasingly shifted from grain to money. But the potter's work in Manupur can only support one family, and there were two traditional potters. The second family, unable to enter agriculture because of its traditional calling and skills, has chosen to move out of Manupur. Four brothers, all unmarried, have left: two have gone to Delhi, one to work for a tailor and one for an electrician; one is in another village, and the fourth has joined the army.

One brother remains in Manupur taking on odd jobs—
from stitching clothes to repairing bicycle tires—and earning a subsistence living. He anxiously awaits the day when
his children will be grown up and his living conditions
improved.

Milkha Singh, then, is the only Ghumar in Manupur
who remains a potter by occupation. He has three sons
and three daughters. The eldest son has emigrated, and in
1970 was looking for a job in the city. He has "education,"
but if he cannot find a job, he will have to return and
perform the work of the "uneducated" in the fields. The
middle son works with a farmer as a crop-sharer and
brings in about 1,500 rupees a year. The youngest is only
ten and is in Grade 5. During vacation, he helps his father
with the pottery. During the school year, he performs odd
jobs for one of his father's former Jat Jajmans. In return,
he earns his meals, clothing, and, according to his father,
"maybe thirty to fifty rupees a year." Milkha Singh's
daughters also work. Every morning they collect dung for
the farmer and carry it to the manure pits in the fields.
In return, they receive that day's meals.

Milkha Singh has no desire to limit the size of his family.
His reaction is again typical of the poor in Manupur: "You
think I am poor because I have too many children. [He
laughs.] If I didn't have my sons, I wouldn't have half the
prosperity I do. And God knows what would happen to
me and their mother when we are too old to work and
earn."*

---

*The issue of security will be discussed in Chapter 6.

Lohar-Tarkhan: A Textbook Case of "Overpopulation"

The occupations of *Lohar* (blacksmith) and *Tarkhan* (carpenter) have traditionally been the preserve of one individual. He used to repair the agricultural tools of his Jajman cultivators, but tools are no longer as simple as they used to be, and the skills of the smith have hardly kept pace with the change in agricultural technology. Chaffing machines are used for both sugarcane and fodder; the tractor is beginning to replace the plough. Some farmers have begun to take their tools into Khanna for repairs; others, faced with the high cost of repairs in town, have begun to learn to make at least minor repairs themselves.

As a result, there is less demand for the services of the smith in Manupur. Hereditary Jajmani relations have dissolved as farmers have taken advantage of the services available in Khanna. The blacksmiths have had to ignore their caste obligations to their fellow smiths in order to compete for what work remains.

The blacksmith might seem to represent an ideal type for the family planner, a textbook case of a group "suffering" from "population pressure": work has decreased while numbers have increased; since work cannot be increased, the equation can only be balanced by reducing their numbers to make them commensurate with the available work. The solution: family planning.

The smith in Manupur doesn't reason this way. I posed the dilemma and the corresponding "solution" to Hakika Singh, who has perhaps suffered most from the drastic decline in smithy work. Today he serves five farmers, as opposed to the fifty or so his father used to serve, and can barely earn a subsistence living. Here is the gist of Hakika Singh's response to my query:

If things stay the same, the farmers will keep on going to Khanna to get their work done. I will lose even what I have. Unless I am to leave this village, I must teach my sons to repair the new machines and maybe even get some machinery [tools] myself. The problem is I have no money, and the Cooperative Society only loans to farmers. So there is only one way out. And that is to have enough sons. Don't smile. If I have sons, they will work outside, labor even as animals do, but save. While the rest work, one son will learn the new skills. And maybe we will even be able to get some machinery with the savings of the other sons. And, you know, if we learn how to do it, there really is enough work in this village.

To Hakika Singh, the solution to his financial troubles is not to reduce the size of the family he has to support, but to *increase* it. It is the family that will support him, will even be his salvation. Admittedly, he must take one chance: the next baby may be a girl instead of a boy. But since he is faced with utter financial disaster if he does anything else, Hakika Singh is willing to take that chance. Even with a number of sons, he may fail; yet they are his only hope. Even if the chances for success are low, his sons are his only route to success. As we concluded our conversation, his parting words were: "A rich man invests in his machines. We must invest in our children. It's that simple."

Darzi and Nai: Large Families for Educational Security

The barber and the tailor can be added to the list of "victims" of the farmer's prosperity. Although traditionally "low" in the caste hierarchy, the *Nai* (barber) and the *Darzi* (tailor) were the most prosperous of the "low" castes in the village. The barber traditionally trimmed the farmer's hair.* He gave haircuts to the Brahmins and cut their fingernails and toenails. His wife shampooed their wives' hair. Now the farmer buys his own razor and his wife buys her shampoo.

The barber was also customarily the messenger sent by the "higher" castes to their relatives in the nearby villages, and he was usually the matchmaker when marriages were arranged. For his services, he received gifts on all the auspicious occasions celebrated by his Jajman families, as well as a stipulated share of the agricultural produce. He was uneducated, though he had contacts with the outside world in his role as matchmaker, which required him to have an intimate knowledge of families in the surrounding villages. In Manupur today, the heads of all four barber families no longer cut hair, but remain as messengers for the Jats, earning barely a quarter of their previous income —which means only meals.

The tailor's earnings came from selling cloth and making clothes for the Brahmins and the farmers. His work brought him in frequent contact with Khanna, where he bought most of his cloth. He thus had to be literate, and he had to have a rudimentary knowledge of accounts. Consequently, his sons usually had at least a grade school education, and he had the material prosperity to ensure it. He also used to be a petty moneylender, but government financing for farmers destroyed all other forms of moneylending in Manupur. The presence of the sewing machine in practically every upper-class household made

---

*All farmers in Manupur are Sikhs. Their religion forbids them from cutting even a single hair from their own bodies. The farmers, however, have always trimmed their own beards. In the hot and humid summer, many even cut away an oval of hair in the center of their heads and wear a turban.

the tailor unnecessary. Of the five heads of tailor families, two are now teachers and one is a cloth salesman in Khanna. The remaining two, the oldest ones, remain as tailors, but both must supplement their incomes through some other form of labor, be it repairing bicycles or selling sweets to children.

Both the tailor and the barber are today involved in a desperate struggle to adjust to the new life and to somehow maintain their traditional income and status. In part, their efforts are aimed at resisting being relegated to working as agricultural laborers, a process which has absorbed most of the other service castes in Manupur. But their only other alternatives are to emigrate or to qualify for a skilled position in the village. A lack of money has ruled out the emigration of the entire family, at least for the present. The parents are therefore determined to acquire marketable skills (meaning an education) for their sons so that *they* can either get a skilled job in the village (such as teaching) or can emigrate to the town.

In this, the Darzi and the Nai are similar to the rest of the service castes in Manupur: they all want to have enough children to accumulate savings. But the case of the tailor and the barber is particularly interesting because it goes against another widely accepted "truth" among family planners: that families who want education, and particularly higher education, for their children will limit their families because higher education is expensive and, therefore, to have many children is expensive. Family planning should thus mean substantial savings and should be a rational decision for these parents.

The tailor and the barber reason exactly the opposite way. To begin with, most families have either little or no savings, and they can earn too little to be able to finance the education of *any* children, even through high school.

Another source of income must be found, and the only solution is, as one tailor told me, "to have enough children so that there are at least three or four sons in the family." Then each son can finish high school by spending a part of his afternoon working for a farmer and earning at least his meals. After high school, one son is sent on to college while the others work to save and pay the necessary fees. During the summer, the college son works and earns at least a part of his expenses. Once his education is completed, he will use his increased earnings to put his brother through college. He will not marry until the second brother has finished his college education and can carry the burden of educating the third brother.

Take the case of Makan Singh, a barber. Makan Singh has five sons and two daughters. One daughter is high-school educated and married; the other is in Grade 8. The three eldest sons have already been educated (one has a B.A. and is a teacher, another has an M.A. and is a teacher, and the third has a B.A. and is a civil servant). Significantly, the third son, though thirty years old, is unmarried. Makan Singh told me emphatically that he will remain unmarried until he has put his younger brother, who is a first-year student, through college. The same responsibility will then fall upon the fourth brother since the youngest, who is now in Grade 7, will then be ready to go to college.

The same thing is happening in Iser Singh's family. The eldest son is an engineering graduate, unmarried at twenty-five, and is financing his younger brother's college education. In fact, among the four families where the children are old enough to be in college (two barbers and two tailors), there are seven college graduates and four now studying in college. Of the graduates, two are unfortunately, unemployed, reflecting the generally high rate of unemployment among the educated in India. (Two factors related to unemployment should be noted: it exists only among the educated in Manupur, and it is a most recent phenomenon in the village.) The fathers interviewed were concerned about this unemployment, hoped it was temporary, and felt that, even so, their only salvation lay in education.

Instances of family planning among the barber and tailor families are rare, and when they do occur, it is only after the family has had "enough" sons. This is in spite of the fact that the heads—not just the sons—of tailor families are among the most educated in the village. For example, Ajaib Singh holds a B.A. and is a teacher in the nearby village. He has recently undergone a vasectomy, but only after having seven children—among them five sons. For them, education, in itself, gives no indication of the response of an individual to the prospect of a small family. As we shall see later, the Brahmins, who are as educated as the tailors, have precisely the opposite attitude toward family planning.

There is one important factor, however, which is beginning to affect the rate of natural increase among these families: the generally very late age at which a son marries (usually in his thirties) will mean that his family will probably be smaller.

The rise in the age of marriage has been particularly marked among the tailors and the barbers, although it has also been the case among the agricultural classes in the village, where technological change has increased the productivity of labor and the work load and, as a result, the marriages of girls are being delayed. What is of interest is that, as the Khanna Study pointed out,[1] it was the rise in the age of marriage—from 17.5 years in 1956 to over 20 in 1969—and not the birth control program that was responsible for the decrease in the birth rate in the

village from 40 per 1,000 in 1957 to 35 per 1,000 in 1968.
While the birth control program was a failure, the net
result of technological and social change in Manupur was
to bring down the birth rate.

The Brahmins: The Declining Aristocracy

Shaktiprasad is a Brahmin. He rests in his sitting room
on the second floor of his house. The view from the window commands a panorama of the entire western side of
the village. He looks out, sighs, and reminisces:

> In this house money was never counted, it was always
> measured [weighed]. My grandfather would bring in
> thousands of rupees a day—they were all silver rupees
> then—and it took too much time to count it. So we
> weighed it.

He leans his head against the wall and rests it in the cup
of his fingers. Once every few minutes, he has to move his
body to catch every waft of the cool breeze that drifts
above the other houses and through his window. The
summer heat is damp, and the breeze means relief from
the humidity. Unlike several of the Jat families, Shaktiprasad does not enjoy the luxury of an electrical fan.

The furniture in the house suggests a glorious past and
a miserable present. The beds are forty years old, ornate,
and sturdy. The wooden wardrobes are built into the wall,
and the doors are skillfully carved, with glass knobs as
handles. But the walls show small cracks, and though the
village was electrified in 1964, Shaktiprasad's house has no
electricity. Oil lamps burn dimly at night and testify to
the fate of the Brahmins in Manupur.

Shaktiprasad's grandfather was, as he said, "no com-
moner." He was the richest man in the district, the major
moneylender, and the most famous Hakim around, one

who could boast of a clientele in twenty villages. As Shaktiprasad told me: "I was the first one in the village to go to a college. No one else could afford it then. We owned half this street. Now we have sold some and have had to divide the rest of the property among our several families."

When a Brahmin in Manupur talks of the recent changes in Manupur, he does not talk about the prosperity of the Jats or the prospects of a better life for most of the village population, but of the "greed and materialism of the Jats," of their "lack of culture and vulgarity," and sometimes of their "exploitation of the Achuta agricultural laborers." Although, on the surface, relations between Brahmins and Jats are polite and civil, beneath it all exists a simmering resentment. Social change has meant progress for the Jats, poverty for the Brahmins. The demands of readjustment have been total and painful. Their effect upon the Brahmin family has been sudden, drastic, and cruel.

The Brahmins estimate that in 1920 there were about fifty Brahmin families in Manupur. Today only sixteen (4.3 percent of the village population) remain. Unlike the tailors and the barbers, the Brahmins had both education and considerable savings. In the face of adversity, immediate emigration was a feasible alternative, and those families which could went to seek work elsewhere. Even the remaining families have been split: the able-bodied have emigrated; the sick, aged, not-so-well-off, and not-so-well-educated have been left behind to struggle to maintain a semblance of their customary status, privilege, and income. This means, as one Brahmin explained, having to "work in un-Brahmin professions." It also means holding a number of jobs at one time, for outside the agricultural economy there are few jobs which can alone provide any more than a bare subsistence.

Table 10
Brahmins and their Occupations

Sector of the economy	Where employed	Occupation	Total for Manupur	Grand total
Agriculture	In Manupur	Farmer	1	2
	Outside	Farm labor (1)		
Commerce and investment	In Manupur	Shopkeeper* (5)	6	7
		Taxi owner and driver (1)		
	Outside	Shopkeeper (1)		
Skilled services (requiring at least a high-school education)	In Manupur	Paramedic Hakim† (1)	1	11
	Outside	Professor (1)		
		Draftsman (2)		
		Radio mechanic (1)		
		Clerk (4)		
		Civil servant (1)		
		Teacher (1)		

---

*One of the shopkeepers is also the postmaster and a Hakim. Also, although there are five Brahmin shopkeepers, there are only four Brahmin shops. The fifth works in his father's shop.

†The Hakim is also a petition writer.

Semiskilled and unskilled services (not requiring a high-school education)	In Manupur	Taxi driver	1	9
	Outside	Storekeeper (1) Cycle repairer (2) Military (3) Policemen (2)		

| Noneconomic activity | | Priest (2) Disabled or retired (3) College students (3) | | |

Of the Brahmin families that remain in Manupur, 35 percent of the earning members work in Manupur and 65 percent work elsewhere. Of those working in Manupur —including the priests—46 percent are shopkeepers.

Dilipchand is Shaktiprasad's brother. He spent four years at home after high school learning the profession of the Hakim, but his medical practice has been considerably reduced since many villagers use the free medical facilities at the government-owned Civil Hospital in Khanna. Dilipchand must now do other work to supplement his income. He runs a shop and also works as the village postmaster. His monthly income is as follows:

Hakim	200 rupees
Shop	40-50 rupees
Post office	50 rupees
Total	290-300 rupees

A monthly income of 290 to 300 rupees is hardly sufficient to support his family of eight, when he must also save for emergencies and future ceremonies such as marriages. Dilipchand considers himself lucky, since he has three sons—two work as clerks in a nearby town and one is in the military—who send him a part of their salaries to supplement the family budget. This is the only way he can meet such expenses as the 500 rupees he had to spend on his mother's funeral ceremony in July and also save a little for the future.

Dilipchand has three daughters. One is twelve years old and was born in 1958. He says he told the Khanna Study he was "using" contraceptives, even though he wasn't. He adds: "If they are happy writing my name, let them do it. Why should it worry me?" In 1960, the year the study ended, he decided to begin abstaining from sexual intercourse and he has practiced abstention since then. He gives two reasons: first, a seventh boy child would only be an added expense since by the time he was old enough to begin earning—not until sixteen or so among the Brahmins, as will be explained later—Dilipchand and his wife would either be dead or too old to gain any benefits; second, he could not take the chance of having one more girl child.

There are nine shops in Manupur. Six belong to the traditional "high" castes (four to Brahmins, one to a Khatri, and one to a Sonar,* two belong to Achutas, and

---

*Traditionally, the *Khatri* was the shopkeeper and the *Sonar* the goldsmith. Under British rule, however, both became moneylenders, as did the Brahmins. The Khatri and the Sonar thus belonged to the same social class and enjoyed the same social status as the Brahmins. Today, of the three heads of Khatri and Sonar families in Manupur, one is single and works as a government family-planning worker,

one to a Nai). For Achutas, participation in the trade sector is an attempt at upward mobility, whereas for the rest, it is a struggle to avoid slipping down the economic ladder.

A shopkeeper has a very small turnover. He saves little or nothing and exists almost on a day-to-day basis. Every two or three days he must send someone or go himself to Khanna to buy his supplies. He can never afford to buy anything in bulk. If he has a son, and every shopkeeper does, the son will tend the shop while the father goes to make the purchases in the town. Another son or daughter —probably both—will tend the buffalo, bring it grass and water, take it to the pond for a wash, etc. None of the shopkeepers can afford to hire someone for this job. Those who do not have children usually do not have any livestock.

Table 11

Ownership of Livestock in Manupur by Caste

Caste	Families	Families with livestock	%
Jats	143	140	97.9
Achutas	61	54	88.5
Nonagricultural "low" service castes	41	30	73.2
Nonagricultural "high" service castes	20	11	55.0
Total	265	235	88.7

and two are shopkeepers. We can thus talk of the two Khatri and Sonar families as "high" caste shopkeepers. As may be expected, their response to social change has been the same as that of the Brahmins, and so is their attitude toward family planning.

The shopkeeper in Manupur works very hard and the hours are long—five in the morning to ten at night. It might be expected that village commerce would reap benefits from the prosperity of the agricultural sector, but this has not been the case. Not only do the farmers grow most of their food, but the Jat-Brahmin hostility and the proximity of Khanna has meant that they buy most of their supplies there. Shops in Manupur usually sell only spices, children's sweets, fresh vegetables, and cooking oil. Most owners—especially those belonging to the "high" castes—hope at best to save enough to educate their sons and make a better life possible for the next generation. As Krishan Lal, a Brahmin shopkeeper told me: "I work eighteen hours a day, from five in the morning to eleven at night. No one else works like this. You think I would want to wish such a life on my son?"

There is a difference between the attitude of the Brahmin and that of the tailor and the barber. Where the tailor is willing to have younger sons work for the farmer or do other menial work so that his elder son can be educated, the Brahmin looks with utter disdain and fear upon the prospect of farm labor. The reasons are implicit in the caste system, which traditionally equated a low social status with menial labor. The Brahmin took pride in the fact that he never touched the earth: physical labor was regarded with contempt, and abstention from it was a matter of honor. Today the Brahmin tries to preserve that same honor. Letting his children work for the farmer— who is lower in the caste hierarchy—would be the clearest admission of the decline of the Brahmin aristocracy.

The traditional nonagricultural "high" castes in Manupur have not only been bypassed, but have also been undermined by the wave of prosperity. Of all the castes, they have gone through the most drastic changes and feel most acutely the uncertainty of the future. As a result, they put tremendous emphasis upon thrift and savings, on the need for financial security for the family and educational security for the children. Their children, both boys and girls, are apt to be the most educated, even beyond high school. Along with the tailors and the barbers, they marry the latest and emigrate the most often. Unlike the tailors and the barbers, however, they are likely to see the greatest advantage in family planning.

Table 12
Education Among Brahmin Children

Descrip-tion	Primary School (Grades 1-5)			Secondary School (Grades 6-10)		
	Total of school age	Total in school	%	Total of school age	Total in school	%
Boys	3	2	67.0	6	4	67.0
Girls	8	7	88.0	13	10	77.0
Total 11		9	82.0	19	14	74.0

The Khanna Study argues that the high rate of net emigration from Manupur represents an effort on the part of the villagers to "solve their population problem." We have seen that the high rate of emigration from Manupur is not spread equally among the castes, but is particularly marked among a few castes, all of them belonging to the nonagricultural service sector. The data gathered by the Khanna Study during the years of its operation support this—although the conclusions are markedly different.

The Khanna Study reports that the "high" castes other than the Jats living in the study area had "a net migration more than twice that of any other group."[2] In Manupur, the most significant among these "high" castes are the Brahmins, and it is true that the number of Brahmin families declined from twenty-six in 1955 to sixteen in 1970. This decline was closely followed by that of the barbers and the tailors, whose families numbered thirteen in 1955,[3] and only nine in 1970.*

This minority of Brahmins, barbers, and tailors is united by a single feature. They represent the traditionally prosperous people of Manupur whose material basis of life was undermined by the rise of the Jat farmer class and the technological changes in the village. They are neither the poorest nor the largest families in Manupur. In fact, in 1959, those who were the poorest and had the largest families in the study area were the Majbis, and they migrated the least.[4] The Chamars had an average net emigration equal to that of the Jats. Both belonged to the agricultural economy. Also, in 1959, though the Majbis were the poorest, only 3 percent of their households received any financial assistance from any male member living and working outside. The comparable figure for Brahmins was 16 percent.

Further, except for the Brahmins, those castes which had a high rate of net emigration considered a large family essential for their survival. And the Brahmins were not alleviating a "population problem" by emigrating, for, as the Khanna Study itself stated, they already had "exceptionally low rates of natural increase."[5] That is to say, they were successfully limiting their families before they began

---

*These figures refer only to *entire* families that have emigrated from Manupur, and so they somewhat underestimate the net emigration because the emigration of individual members of the family is omitted.

to emigrate. To view the high rate of emigration as an attempt to alleviate "population pressure" or to solve the "population problem," as the Khanna Study does, is to misunderstand the reality. The fact is that emigration in the study area was a socioeconomic variable, not a demographic one.

In this chapter, we have attempted to understand the response of various nonagricultural service castes in Manupur to technological changes in the village. The response to social change results from the position a class holds in the social order and the perception it has of the opportunities open to it within that order. That is why, when faced with the same situation, the poor respond differently from the rich, the marginally prosperous arrive at a solution different from that of the wealthy. And so, in Manupur, those who had few resources responded to adversity not by decreasing their numbers, but by increasing them. In numbers they found security and the only opportunity for prosperity.

Notes

1. *The Khanna Study,* pp. 298, 300.
2. Ibid., p. 215.
3. *Pilot Study,* p. 60.
4. *The Khanna Study,* p. 212.
5. Ibid., p. 215.

6

The Family

The struggle for survival and continued existence occupies the better part of an individual's time in Manupur. There exists an urgency and immediacy about material interests that cannot escape even the casual visitor. Even though a little prosperity has come to Manupur within the last decade or so, for most farmers this has only meant that they can have three complete meals a day. While technological change has increased the productivity of their land and labor, it has also made intensive agriculture possible and increased their work load.

Work is hard as well as time-consuming, and distractions are few and far between. Time is never allocated separately for work and for leisure: leisure is enjoyed only when the rains make it impossible to work, rest is possible only when fatigue demands it. There are no weekends; every day is a potential workday. In Manupur, life *is* work.

The rains may interrupt the activity of the men, especially the farmers, but not of the women. In fact, when a woman's husband is at home, he demands much more, and her work is increased. The major interruption in her work is pregnancy, but she assumes her normal work load up to the last three weeks of pregnancy and then limits herself to domestic work. Help is hired to do the outside work (for instance, tending the cattle) or a relative comes and helps. The woman stops work completely only a few hours before the birth; her confinement lasts no more than a week.

All but the very young and the very old make some productive contribution to the economy of the household. Older women spend their time spinning cotton into thread, a task which requires little physical labor and can be accomplished in short sittings. The thread is spun for the household or for someone who will pay for it in either money or grain.

Young girls, even when they go to school, spend their afternoons weaving mats. They make several patterns in colorful designs. A few will be used to decorate the house, while others will be sold in the village or in Khanna. Those that cannot be sold will be kept for the child's dowry. In their "free" time, young girls try to find paying tasks so that they can earn as much of their dowry as possible.

With work a total concern, even the few traditional distractions—such as festivals—have diminished in importance. Whereas the two important festivals of *Tij* and *Janmashtmi* were previously celebrated by the entire village, today only children take time out for rejoicing. Adults and young people simply add a few sweet dishes to the meal at the end of the day. In the same way, the number of visits paid to relatives outside the village (to the wife's family, for example) has been drastically curtailed. What were previously considered important social obligations have been reduced to polite social conventions. The most painful and direct effect has been on the aged. An old woman who was, as far as she could remember, in her late eighties or early nineties complained of the change, but with resignation: "Neglected today are grandparents, wells, and cows."

The family structure in Manupur is rigidly patriarchal and authoritarian. The father is the head of the family and exercises absolute control. In practice his authority might be shared to some degree, depending upon the family, with his wife, but he is at the top and the children are at the bottom. The child-parent relationship is simple: the parent commands, the child obeys. Age and experience are the yardsticks of merit and the claim to authority. A young child, however absorbed he or she may be in any form of play, will instantly stop at the most casual command of the parent.

An older man—and in Manupur that means one past his forties—who has a number of children in the house is assured a certain ease in life. When he returns from work, whatever the work may be, his youngest one will massage his head and feet, or his body, if it aches. He will bring water for a wash and a bath, and if it is very hot or humid, he will make lemon-sugar juice. Children perform a variety of small tasks that adults regard as tedious, time-consuming, and tiresome. Once in a while, a man without any small children will be seen carrying his own water from the pump or the well and cursing his fate for not having bestowed enough children upon him. Whether you are rich or poor, you are ensured these small luxuries if you have enough children.

Since the children's activity can be of considerable gain to the family, their time and their life are closely regulated by the family, more so as they become older. A young child is pampered and loved, all his needs catered to, until he is about six years old. The transition may begin at five, or even four, when children begin taking care of their younger brothers or sisters, but by six, the attitude of the elders and the life of the child have changed completely.

Older children take care of the younger ones, include them in their play, take them out in the fields in the morning and evening to be relieved, carry them on their hips when doing work, such as grazing animals. A young girl is often seen taking her younger brother or sister to school with her. Although the younger one is not old enough to attend, she takes him so she can take care of him. The school adjusts to the needs of the society, as does every institution in the village.

Darshana Kumari is thirteen years old and a student in Grade 8. Her day begins at five in the morning when she gets up and makes the morning tea. Then she walks to the fields to relieve herself, taking the buffalo dung out to the dung pots. School lasts from 7:30 to 1:30. The next hour and a half is devoted to school work and the rest of the day, from 3:30 to 9:00 in the evening, is taken up with various household duties. Darshana's primary responsibility is taking care of the one buffalo. She takes it out for cleaning, grazing, and drinking. In the evening she milks it and sets some aside for making tea, a little more for making yoghurt, and the rest for making butter. After dinner she washes the dishes. Twice a week—on Sunday and Wednesday—she spends two hours washing her school clothes. Three years ago, at the age of ten, Darshana Kumari stopped spending her evenings playing with her girl friends in the village fields. Why? "Because I had grown up. Only young ones play."

There is no adolescence in Manupur. There is only childhood and adulthood. The young in Manupur seldom display the carefree, spontaneous attitude that industrial society proverbially associates with youth. Children learn

that if they are to be part of the family, they must contribute to it. Thus, children grow, not into youths, but into
young adults.

The claim of the family on the lives of its children is
total. Parents arrange the marriages of their children, and
marriages are really a liaison between families: the primary factor is the economic position of the other family.

The fact that the family is the basic unit of work has
important social implications. The discipline of work is
reflected in the discipline of the family. The family is the
most effective institution for maintaining discipline in
society, and there are good reasons why the individual
submits to family discipline. It should be clear from the
discussion in the last two chapters that for an overwhelming majority in Manupur the financial enterprise which is
its unit of work is a family enterprise and, therefore, its
source of economic security. Even for those who do not
work, the young and the aged, the family is the source of
economic security. When a couple grows too old to work,
their only shelter is among their children, and parents
have a socially approved claim on the resources of their
children. When no children have survived or none were
born—most unusual, in either case—the parents continue
to live in the family home and survive on the charity
handed out by relations or other caste members. Life
under such circumstances is said to be "a curse" and "most
degrading."

Since daughters must always marry outside the village,
security for old age depends solely on the number of sons
a couple has. It is impossible for them to go and live in
their daughter's household since strong social taboos prevent even the contemplation of such a possibility. No
father may take anything free from his daughter, and no
brother from his sister. It is even inadmissible for a parent

to spend a single night in the village where his married daughter lives.

The family also provides almost the only form of physical security. In Manupur, there are no police, or any other form of legally organized force. All conflicts theoretically go to the village Panchayat, which has the power to arbitrate such matters. The Panchayat, however, has no way to implement its decisions unless it calls upon law enforcement authorities from Khanna. Most important, the absence of a legally organized force means that the Panchayat has little power to maintain public peace in the community.

Most conflicts in Manupur, whether between individuals or groups, fall into two general categories. A large number start among the farmers and usually have their origin in the nature of land holdings in the village. Since most holdings are very, very small, the farmers jealously guard every bit of their territory against encroachment from neighboring cultivators. At ploughing time the possibility always exists that a farmer, tending the edge of his plot, may expropriate a tiny piece of adjacent territory by merely taking the plough a few steps too far.

Other conflicts occur between farmer and farm laborer. Because of the seasonal shortage of laborers, and the corresponding rise in their money wages and bargaining power, relations between the farmer and his labor force are often rather strained. The Achutas increasingly refuse to perform their customary Jajmani obligations—such as carrying away dead animals—for the Jats. The Jats, in turn, consider the Achutas "uppity" or maintain that their "new-found power has gone to their heads." Since Achutas comprise by far the majority of the agricultural labor force, there is little that the Jats can do to harm their collective position. In the long run, of course, both know that mechanization will be the final arbiter, and in the favor of farmers, at that. But in the short run, it is not unusual for a Jat farmer—especially one of those who can barely make ends meet—to single out a particular laborer, usually one with a small family and few relatives, for physical punishment.

But most conflicts in Manupur are not resolved through a resort to physical violence. In fact, it is estimated that close to 90 percent of all conflicts are settled through arbitration by the Panchayat. These include most minor conflicts and most intercaste conflicts.

The five members of the Panchayat are elected by vote of the entire community. The law stipulates that one of these must be an Achuta; the other four have always been Jats since the Jats are numerically the majority—nearly 60 percent—and exercise most of the economic power in the village. As a political organization, the Panchayat reflects the real distribution of power in the village and is an instrument of Jat dominance, defending the interests of the farmers. The Achuta is a "token" member. When the Panchayat arbitrates a conflict between a Jat and a non-Jat, the Jat will usually win.

Serious intracaste conflicts, which are between farmers, do not as a rule come to the Panchayat. They are solved by the two "factions" through the use of force—sticks, knives, swords, and sometimes guns*—and in the course of the fight, it is not uncommon for at least one person to be killed. Numbers become very important on such occasions.

---

*Jats who were once members of the armed forces usually own a firearm. A few other farmers may also own guns.

A family is not involved in such a quarrel every year, and may never be in the course of a lifetime. But every family knows that if it is to be realistic, it must anticipate such an occasion and prepare for it. It also knows that the fewer able-bodied males there are in the house, the more attractive a target it will be. Not that the courts in Khanna are not open to the people of Manupur, or the police inaccessible; but both are far away and neither is present in case of a reprisal. Besides, honor is involved. If feuds do go to the courts or to the police, it is only *after* the factions have resorted to force.

The need to guarantee physical security for the members of the family thus becomes one more reason parents look favorably on having a large family. Here is but one example. Puran Singh is in his fifties and has been witness or party to a number of these fights; they are a significant part of his "reality." He praises God for giving him many sons, for sons bring prosperity, peace, and honor. He told me he hoped I realized that his sons were responsible for the fact that he was still alive. He scoffed at the idea of using contraceptives and added: "In these villages we have faction fights, and you win fights not with contraceptives but with men."*

The factions that Puran Singh talked of have long been a feature of village life, but the social composition of these factions has changed as the social conditions in the village have changed. Previously, each faction was a *thola*,

---

*By 1970, this statement must have assumed the status of a "saying" in Manupur, for Dr. Wyon of the Khanna Study recalled having heard it from one of the villagers. This also indicates that the Khanna Study directors were not totally oblivious to the socioeconomic factors that affect the decision to have children, even though they apparently did not consider them very important.

a collection of extended families, all related by blood.* The decline of the thola as a political institution has paralleled the decline of social ownership. The thola was based on one or another form of social property (even if it coexisted with private property) and on blood relations; the village is now a market society where private property dominates, and the faction is the *dhala,* a grouping of individual families which cuts across clan lines. Its members cooperate economically, are bound by social and ceremonial ties, and form a political alliance during village elections. When a joint family breaks up into two separate enterprises, each may join a different faction.

Although many villagers say the thola declined in importance as people became educated and less adverse to forming alliances across blood lines, dhala alliances are not in fact confined to the educated. The change has followed a change in economic organization—as the unit of work became less the joint family and more the semi-joint or nuclear family.

For the poor in Manupur, emergencies come not only as fights, but also as natural disasters. The most frequent emergency comes during the monsoon season when as many as three or four houses may be destroyed by the heavy rains. These are the dried-mud *Kacha* houses, the weakest ones, the homes of the poor, which account for about 40 percent of the village. One victim of the rains one night in the summer of 1970 was Daulat, the drum beater. The next morning I found him squatting in front

---

*The *thola* corresponds to the anthropologist's conception of a clan. It also corresponds to the *dhars* Oscar Lewis talks of in his study of village Rampur in Delhi state (see Oscar Lewis, *Village Life in Northern India* [Urbana: University of Illinois Press, 1958], pp. 113-154).

of the rubble that was once his house, as his wife collected their few belongings and tended their two young children. He lamented: "Look at my home. It has been wrecked by the rains. If I had enough people in my family, we could put it back together. Now I shall have to hire laborers to do it and that means putting a bandage on my stomach for quite some time to come."

When confronted with an emergency, and this includes physical violence, a villager can be fairly certain that his family members will support him, regardless of the merit of his position. This has "always been the case," and there is very good reason for it to be so. The family in Manupur is not only a group linked by ties of blood, but also by ties of money. The family is a financial enterprise, and a threat to a family member is also a threat to the family enterprise. What has changed, however, is that the relevant family unit is less often the joint family and more often the nuclear family.

We have seen again and again how children—especially sons—are vital to the people of Manupur. And so it is to be expected that religion, myth, tradition, and ritual will reinforce the belief in this necessity. A variety of mediums—song, story, proverb, or even the mere explanation of phenomena—are used for this purpose. The message transmitted is always the same: it is one's *Dharma* (religious and social obligation) to have children: to desire as many children as possible is not only in the natural order of things but also an indication of virtue.

Perhaps the most frequent and confusing experience an outsider has in a society such as Manupur's is the confrontation with an individual who in the course of a single conversation will go back and forth between a sober analysis and a seemingly superstitious evocation of divine or cultural aphorisms. The outsider presses for "rational" explanations; he receives a generous dose of "myth" or "superstition." The outsider sighs and shakes his head, as if to say: "Not again." The scenario is played out. The "intellectual" will go home, and the "peasant," "impenetrable" and "superstitious," will remain.

Here are some examples from my own experiences of the use of aphorisms as a response. Hakika Singh and I spent the first half hour exchanging pleasantries, gossip, and jokes. The conversation then shifted to my work and to the number of children he had. After a mostly unsuccessful half hour of prodding him to explain why, despite having five children, he didn't use contraceptives, I asked rather brashly: "But why do you need any more than five children?" He responded: "A fireplace is never satisfied with the fuel it's given. A mother is never satisfied with the sons she has."

On another occasion, early one morning around half-past five when everybody takes a walk to the field to relieve themselves and then congregates in small groups near the three village gates, "grandfather" was contentedly puffing on his water pipe. He beckoned me a little closer and said in his customarily hoarse whisper, "Son, what is all this talk about having no children? Children are a gift from God. It is for us to welcome them, not to kill them."

Jagir Kaur, who has six daughters and one son, once said that even if she wanted to, she wouldn't use family planning, for she would then "violate the solemn promise of Sulakhini to the Guru." Totally mystified, I admitted ignorance and asked her to enlighten me. She explained as follows:

> Sulakhini was married into Manupur with great fanfare. Her happiness lasted for only a short period, for she bore no sons, no children. She cursed her fate, gave to the

poor, and prayed to God, but to no avail. One day a Guru was passing by on his horse. He heard Sulakhini's sad tale and decided to help. Not wishing to seem greedy, she asked for one son. The Guru consented, and proceeded to write the number "one" on a sheet of paper. At that very moment, however, the horse moved and the Guru mistakenly wrote "seven." Once written, fate can never be reversed. So the Guru asked Sulakhini to keep one son and send the other six to him. Sulakhini begged that she be allowed to keep them all, one to till the land, another to look after the animals, a third to look after the house, and so on. The Guru consented. So it is that we in Manupur must take care of all the children we get, or else the wrath of the Guru will be upon us.

Jagir Kaur is a farmer's wife. She *needs* more than the one son she has. But to explain why she has many children she invokes the "solemn promise of Sulakhini to the Guru," thereby following the time-honored practice of making a virtue of necessity.

The marriage system in Manupur is exogamous. The husband stays within the village; the wife, though from the same caste, must come from outside the village. From her first day in the village, she is subtly pressured into accepting the needs of the family as more important than her personal needs, as her major and overriding obligation. She must consider herself first and foremost a mother, a source of labor power for the family. When she enters her husband's house, she touches her mother-in-law's feet with her fingers, signifying obedience and respect. Her mother-in-law responds: "May you have seven sons!" As she enters the house and greets her husband's relatives and the caste elders, they each have the same customary response: "Bathe in milk and you will have lots of sons." Folk songs, usually sung on occasions such as marriage, childbirth, or the harvest, sing the praises of the prolific mother and the fertile soil. A popular theme running through many stories is the love of the mother for the son; it is considered the purest form of human love. The mother who sacrifices for her son is said to perform the noblest sacrifice. The emphasis is upon motherhood as the supreme virtue and the most satisfying role for a woman. The message is clear: her *Dharma* is to bear children, preferably sons.

Neither is society content with exercising mere social pressure. Severe penalties are imposed on the "barren" wife, and this includes not merely women who have no children, but women who have no sons. Discussing why a mother sometimes gives birth to a female and not a male baby, an Achuta mother commented: "It is written in Guru Nanak's *Granthsaheb* [the holy book of the Sikhs] that if you have bad Karma you get more girls than boys."* The *Karma* referred to here is that of the wife, not of the husband. A "barren" wife is a disgrace to the family; she is a bad omen, and she is treated accordingly. To some, she is even a "witch" who can cast evil spells, especially upon children. She can never attend the birth of a child or its celebration, and she is barred from participation in many other happy occasions. Childlessness is the main reason for divorce, and the only socially acceptable justification for polygamy.

Birth control advocates have often argued that since it is the wife who usually suffers the most from having many children (from the effects on her health of a lack of adequate spacing, from the increased demand on her time, and so on), she ought to be supplied with contraceptives she can use without her husband's knowledge. But even

---

*Needless to say, there is no such reference in the *Granthsaheb*.

if the wife wants to limit the number of births, or to space them adequately, the social penalties for "barrenness" are sufficiently severe and often emphasized enough to stop even the most determined woman from following such a path.

The preference for a son over a daughter is clear, and tradition reinforces this too. It is often asserted that boys are conceived on moonlit nights, girls on dark ones. A boy is said to be conceived if sexual intercourse takes place in the first half of the night when the man is stronger, a girl if it takes place in the second half of the night when the woman is stronger.

Female infanticide, although said today to be non-existent, was once a common practice among Punjab villagers. Even today, the preferential treatment of male over female clearly shows in the much higher infant death rate among females and in the resulting higher ratio of males over females in the general population.[1] (In most other parts of the world, females of a general population have lower death rates than males.) As the Khanna Study pointed out:

> Girls less than two years old had a substantially smaller chance of survival than boys of the same age; they died from the same causes, their mothers started them on solid food at the same age as boys, but their parents gave boys higher quality medical care . . . and possibly more supplementary food.[2]

As we might expect, the ratio of males to females is highest among those castes which have the greatest need for sons in their work, and is less high among the others. In the Khanna Study area, the preponderance of males over females is particularly marked among the farmers

(1231:1000) and the least marked among other "high" service castes (1069:1000).[3]*

Celebrations are kept to a minimum at the birth of a girl, but are particularly joyous if the child born is a boy. Furthermore, certain celebrations are held only after the birth of a son. The first occurs thirteen days after birth, when mango leaves are hung at the entrance of the house and a priest is invited for a meal. He sprinkles "holy" water on the mother and the male child to "purify and protect" them. Another similar celebration is held a year later. In addition, the Jajmani "clients" of the higher castes were traditionally given a gift only upon the birth of a son. And most important, the funeral pyre of a father must be lit by his son. The birth of a female child seems an occasion for silent mourning, that of a male child one for public rejoicing.

It should be emphasized that the purpose here is neither to give a static quality to the emerging picture nor to overemphasize the importance of social customs and beliefs. It is quite possible that even when society in Manupur changes, many of the songs, stories, proverbs, and customs described above will remain. At the same time,

---

*The preponderance of male over female babies among farmers had important implications for the institution of marriage in Manupur. When the babies came of age, the males among them far exceeded the females. The practice of polyandry developed in response to this dilemma. Only one brother married; the others shared his wife, and all tilled the land jointly. Polyandry was, by and large, confined to the poorest farmers in Manupur, to those who could promise the least "happiness" in marriage to a prospective bride. Today, however, female babies have a better chance of survival than in the past, and the preponderance of males is not as marked. As a result, more men in the village can find wives, and polyandry has diminished in importance.

new ones will be created, ones that respond to the needs of a different society. Myth and tradition tend to survive even beyond the point of their social usefulness, but, at any point in time, there exists a measure of unity between belief and practice. It is that unity, the reinforcement belief lends to practice, that we have attempted to examine here.

Notes

1. *The Khanna Study*, p. 194.
2. Ibid., p. 195.
3. Ibid., p. 251, Table 33. This data refers to the Test and Control A population.

7
How the Villagers See Birth Control

We have seen that life in Manupur is not the same for everyone. For the overwhelming majority (nearly 95 percent) participating directly or indirectly in the agricultural economy, a large family is a necessity. For the small minority, living under radically different material conditions—teachers, government workers (mostly for family planning), and ex-moneylenders—the importance of children is considerably less. The perceptions the villagers have of birth control are essentially the perceptions of these two groups.

The majority in Manupur found it difficult to believe that the Khanna Study had actually come to introduce contraceptive practices. Even though the Khanna Study was a reality obvious to all, even though its staff lived in the village for a number of years, and even though the whole enterprise "must have cost an incredible amount of money," the majority of the villagers never understood why so much money and effort were being spent on family planning when "surely everybody knows that children are a necessity in life." This belief is the only point of unity

144

among what may otherwise seem a variety of bizarre and confused perceptions.

The villagers' reaction was to attempt to "explain" the Khanna Study in terms that would be more "rational" than merely wanting to limit the size of families. Most of these explanations are sprinkled throughout the reports of the Khanna Study. The study politely calls them "cultural misunderstandings."

The 1955 *Progress Report* referred to this issue and expressed concern that "various rumors had circulated that *the real reasons* for the study were variously for levying more taxes, for missionary work or for foreign intervention."[1] Another study report for the same period mentioned rumors that "members of the staff were spies . . . agents for reestablishing British rules or instituting American rule, . . . or that we were going to destroy the village and rebuild it with straight streets!"[2]*

The villagers searched for "the clue" to what the Khanna Study was "really doing." Every detail of what the study members did was watched suspiciously. One report states: "Serious difficulties sometimes have attended seemingly minor matters. Despite careful preparation of the village authorities, mapping of the village gave rise to uncontrollable rumors of a rise in taxes, another war, or that the village was to be moved."[3]

The Khanna Study conscientiously searched for "cultural factors" that might have led to this "misunderstanding." The most obvious seemed the presence in the village of an Englishman as the study spokesman, and so "the task of explaining our work and motives was delegated to the as-

---

*The government had built a "model village," laid out like a checkerboard about twenty miles from Manupur. The villagers had heard of it and feared their fate might be the same.

sistant field director, himself a Sikh and a Punjabi."[4] There was little improvement. The shock came when the Exploratory Investigations ended after eighteen months of work in a single village. In the words of that same Punjabi assistant field director: "When we were leaving Chakohi after one and a half years of work, I said to the leaders of the village: 'I hope you understand our work in the last eighteen months.' We were told that we had been making frantic efforts to turn them on the side of America and not go to Russia!"[5]

The rumors were not confined to one village or to one period in the history of the operations of the study. The 1958 Pilot Study report lamented:

> All sorts of rumors began flying around, just as they had in the Exploratory Study and in spite of the fact that this time the work was done by Punjabis rather than by the English field director. Some of the opinions of the village folk voiced during February to our male workers are given here:
> 1. You are government overseers come to pull down the houses and make the streets straight.
> 2. You wish to close down the factories of child-making.
> 3. You are to collect taxes or recruit for the army.
> 4. Why could not British doctors have worked for our good when the British were ruling? Why do they begin now?[6]

To the directors of the Khanna Study, all this was evidence of a communications problem: that the "right" leaders had not been contacted, that the "right" kind of information had not been given out. Yet it is clear that there were no leaders, that the whole enterprise seemed fantastic to almost everybody. Furthermore, it was precisely the "right" kind of information—stating that birth control and family planning were the "real" purposes of the Khanna Study—that the people found most incredible. It should be no surprise that an increased dosage of the same did little to benefit the study. Thus, the Pilot Study report concluded: "Suspicion remained our worst enemy throughout, though as time went on the village people did come to trust us more."[7]

As time went on, many of the villagers did come to believe that the Khanna Study was there to promote family planning. The responses then fell into three categories. One group displayed an air of amused tolerance which was typified by the weaver who told me he thought the "outsiders" were just plain "ignorant." Then there were those who were genuinely puzzled about the motives of the study. Consider the following inquiry, one that I encountered several times during my stay in Manupur: "It's strange they offered to give free medicine to stop women from bearing children, but had nothing to help those who could not bear children. That's where medicine could be of use to us."

The final response represented a rather serious charge leveled at the study. A Jat farmer, gently stroking his young son's hair, told me: "These Americans are enemies of the smile on this child's face. All they are interested in is war or family planning."

To be sure, there are people in Manupur who will echo the arguments of the "outsider." These people maintain that the farmer "should" be afraid of land fragmentation and should thus limit his family, that he should realize that "population pressure" exists and should thus be motivated to use family planning. They then explain the hostility of the agricultural population to family planning with the all-too-often-heard escape clause: "They are ignorant, you know." Those who think this way come either from among the few who own large and mechanized farms or from those who are outside of the agricultural economy: a teacher, a family-planning worker, or an ex-moneylender. They either forget, or do not realize, that their own material circumstances have led them to limit their families. Although they live in Manupur, they share the prejudices of the Khanna Study directors and a majority of its staff. It is here that the *class* basis of perceptions becomes evident.

One man was an exception to this class prejudice in Manupur. He was Pandit Pritamdasji, a fifty-year-old Brahmin who worked as a clerk at the school, an "educated" man who had left the village in pre-independence days to fight with the Indian National Army against the British colonial government. In one of our many discussions, he said: "Africa has on the average 90 persons per square mile, very little population, and no "population pressure." Yet it is poor. We are not poor because of our numbers. The reason is another. . . ."

What this reason is penetrates much deeper into the structure of Indian society than this essay can go.

Notes

1. *Progress Report, 1955*, p. 17. Emphasis mine.
2. *Exploratory Investigations I*, pp. 35-36.
3. *Progress Report, 1955*, p. 5.
4. *Exploratory Investigations I*, p. 36.
5. Interview with Dr. Sohan Singh (July 8, 1970).
6. *Pilot Study*, pp. 18-19.
7. Ibid., p. 31.

Appendix:
The Weapon of Statistics

An operational problem that a long-term project promoting technological change must contend with is that of the short-run evaluation of its performance. The question of evaluation is a sensitive one, and the danger of subjectivity is ever present. For the Khanna Study, the way out of this dilemma was to define a "target" population—that segment of the population whose behavior a project is trying to affect directly—and to consider the change in the behavior of the target as an indicator of the success of the program. But even the definition of the target presents problems.

First, at any given time in a population, there are women who are either pregnant, have not begun menstruating after conception, or have no children. It is possible that they may temporarily not feel a "need" for the use of contraception. One question for a birth control project which is evaluating its performance on the spot is whether it should consider the responses of these women when evaluating its impact.* Should the target be defined to include all or any of these women? The decision to use a particular definition has considerable implications for the evaluation of a birth control program. To a great extent, the definition used determines how "good" the result is that follows. Depending on the particular classification used, one can have a high, low, or an intermediary rate of performance for the program.

For the Khanna Study, this question was of enormous significance. The life of the study was contingent upon its "success" in the field, and this "success" depended upon the behavior of the target. The target, however, could be expanded or limited depending upon the classification the study used. There were several alternatives. As is clear from the following list, the Khanna Study exhausted all the classifications it could possibly have used to expand and contract its target.

Definition 1: Fertile Women

>Nonsterile married women between the ages of fifteen and forty-four.
>
>>1. "Crude rate" for fertile wives (total number of fertile women).
>>2. "Corrected rate" for fertile wives (crude rate less pregnant women).

Definition 2: Eligible Women

>The term "eligible" was used to define four different categories of women at different times.

---

*The problem only exists in the short run. In the long run, the only valid indicator of the success of a birth control program is the extent to which it is instrumental in reducing the birth rate in a given population. This is determined by comparing the decline in the birth rate in the study population with that in a control population, where there is no such program.

1. Nonsterile wives between the ages of fifteen and forty-four, less those who are pregnant.[1] (It will be noticed that this is the same as the "corrected rate" for fertile women.)
2. "Corrected rate" for fertile wives less those "desiring to conceive a child."[2]
3. "Corrected rate" for fertile wives less those lactating.[3]
4. "Corrected rate" for fertile wives less (a) women in postpartum amenorrhea (not having resumed menstruation after giving birth) and (b) those desiring to conceive a child.[4]

Definition 3: Totally Eligible Women

Women who were pregnant, in postpartum amenorrhea, or desiring a child were considered "ineligible," but only temporarily so. They were asked whether they would accept contraceptives once they became "eligible," that is, once they began menstruating. Their responses were added to those for "eligible" wives. The Khanna Study termed this category "eligible women and ineligibles expressing a desire for contraception after the reason for ineligibility is removed."[5] In order to minimize the confusion, I have termed the category "totally eligible."

Now let us consider the results from the Exploratory village of Chakohi. By 1955, 107 wives, 115 husbands, and 105 couples had been offered contraception by the staff.[*] Of these, 31 wives, 26 husbands, and 18 couples had accepted.[6] This state of affairs was expressed in two ways:[7]

---

[*]What this means is that 105 wives and 105 husbands—that is 105 couples—had been offered contraceptives. In addition, 2 wives (but not their husbands), and 10 husbands (but not their wives) were also offered contraception. Therefore, in sum, 105 couples, 107 women and 115 men had been offered contraception.

Crude rate of acceptance where wife was fertile

For wives	28.8 percent
For husbands	22.7
For couples	17.1

Corrected rate of acceptance where wife was fertile

For wives	38.4 percent
For husbands	28.0
For couples	22.4

It is obvious that there are differing rates for wives, husbands, and couples and that any of these rates taken separately would be misleading. The Khanna Study directors, however, seldom gave all three rates together; neither did they always give the rates for the same groups in their many communications. The rates usually referred to wives and, infrequently, to couples.

The above rates are only for "fertile" wives. The range is much wider when the categories "eligible" and "totally eligible" are included. Thus when 31 of 107 wives (married, between the age of fifteen and forty-four, and not sterile) accepted contraception, this result was expressed in the following terms in various communications:[*]

Crude rate of acceptance for fertile wives	28.8 percent
Corrected rate of acceptance for fertile wives	38.4
Rate of acceptance for eligible wives	48.0
Rate of acceptance for totally eligible wives	65.0

Depending upon the classification used, the rate of acceptance in the Exploratory village of Chakohi in March 1955 could be, and was, expressed as anywhere from 28.8 percent to 65.0 percent.

Since the Khanna Study had few precedents, it would

---

[*]For sources of all figures quoted from hereon in this chapter, please consult Table A and footnotes to the Table.

be reasonable to expect some methodological problems to be resolved only in practice. We would expect the study, in the course of its field work, to learn the disadvantages of a particular classification and discard it in favor of another; but such was not the case. One particular classification was never systematically dropped in favor of another. Not only did the Khanna Study use different classifications at different times, but it used different classifications when writing of the same situation to different people.

The information the Khanna Study gathered on its own performance was of interest to three different groups. Of immediate importance was the Advisory Committee, which "advised" the Rockefeller Foundation and the government of India whether or not to continue making financial contributions. The second group was the interested public, including outside specialists in birth control and demography. And, finally, of course, there were the directors who formulated policy and the staff who carried out the day-to-day work of the project.

Communications about the study came from a single source. They were compiled by the field director, Dr. John Wyon, and were usually written by the study director, Dr. John Gordon. Dr. Wyon both compiled and wrote the reports to the staff.[8] Both men prepared separate communications, each directed at a different group. Yearly progress reports and special reports went to the Advisory Committee. They were short, six to twelve pages, and were written in an informal style. Their purpose was to justify the continuation of the study. The Advisory Committee also received lengthy reports on the two Exploratory Studies and the Pilot Study—132, 279, and 371 pages, respectively. They received them, however, only after all the major financial contributions to the Khanna Study had been committed. Thus, Exploratory Investigations I was completed in March 1955, but its report wasn't issued until October 1956.[9] Although some of their contents were included in the yearly progress reports and the special reports, these study reports had no bearing on the decisions made by the Advisory Committee.

These detailed reports, however, were of considerable assistance to the directors and the staff in gaining a comprehensive understanding of the behavior of the study population. Specific and short communications were also circulated among the staff at irregular intervals, such as when a difficulty arose. Finally, the project directors prepared *The Khanna Study*, which was aimed at the interested public.

It is important to examine these various forms of different communications, for each gives a radically different interpretation of the six years of field experience. Moreover, the nature of the information transmitted is a function in each case of the importance of the particular group and its relationship to the study.

Table A shows the varying interpretations presented to the three audiences on the impact of the entire field study (from July 1954 to April 1960). It will be noticed that the use of a variety of definitions produces radically different rates for any one month. Examination reveals a certain consistency in the use of these definitions. Reports directed to the staff gave the least optimistic rates.* The rates of performance reported to the Advisory Committee were almost always the highest and consistently conveyed

---

*The only exception to this is the first general impression regarding the receptivity of the population to contraception in July 1954; 90 percent of the people were then said to favor contraception in general.

a desirable situation. For example, the report of Exploratory Investigations I gave 38.4 percent as the corrected rate of acceptance for fertile wives in March 1955. That same month the *Progress Report* sent to the Advisory Committee stated that 48.0 percent of eligible and 65.0 percent of totally eligible wives accepted contraception.

There is one exception to this pattern, but it is only an apparent exception. In a table attached to the April 1956 report to the Advisory Committee, the March 1955 figure is given as 28.8 percent of women accepting. This is part of a sequence, however, which shows 80.9 percent of wives accepting in November 1954, 28.8 percent in March 1955, and 42.0 percent in April 1956. Thus the conclusion: "Acceptability increases, showing the effect of long-term health education. Initial acceptability is not a flash in the pan."[10] The purpose is clearly to show, not just that the population is receptive to contraceptive practice, but that its receptivity is closely related to the work of the Khanna Study. The need of the moment was for a rising trend in acceptance, not a consistently high one. The moral, then: the study works. This would seem to explain why the directors chose to use two different definitions in their communications to the Advisory Committee when presenting rates for March 1955. Both rates were used to make different points.

One of the two aims of the Pilot Study was to test the "effectiveness" of the foam tablets as a method of contraception.[11] At the Advisory Committee meeting on April 3, 1956, the foam tablets were indeed pronounced "effective": "Result. Fifty percent reduction in pregnancy rate of acceptors against the whole control population."[12] The sole evidence was Table 2, which is reproduced in its entirety as Table B. It will be noticed that all the table does is *compare* the pregnancy rate of the acceptors against

Table A[*]

Communication directed to	Exploratory I and II								
	1954			1955			1956		
	July	Sept.	Nov.	Feb.	March	Oct.	March	April	
Staff	90% in favor of contraception[1]				fertile wives: 38.4% corrected rate of acceptance[2]		fertile wives: 46.6% corrected rate of acceptance[3]		wi... 17... use...
Advisory Committee		wives accept: 57% el. 76% totally el.[9]	80.9% wives accept[10]	wives accept: 57% el. 76% totally el. husbands accept: 40% el. 78% totally el.[11]	wives accept: 48% el. 65% totally el.[12] 28.8% wives accept[10]		eligible: wives 46% husbands 40% couples 39% accept and use[13]	42% wives accept[10]	
Interested public							fertile couples: 24% accept foam tablets[20]		

*Notes to the Table will be found at the end of the Appendix. The rates in italic were issued "in retrospect"—that is, at least a year after their date of reference. "El." refers to eligible.

Table A—Continued

Pilot		Definitive Study							
55		1956		1957			1958	1959	1960
pt.	Oct.	March	April	April	Oct.	Nov.	March	March	April
s:		wives: 13% use[4]				acceptance well below 25%[5]	Use rate evidently ...10%[8] Use rate ... about 15%[7] 12% of all husbands and wives use[6]		
	eligible: wives 30% husbands 39% couples 29% accept and use[14]	wives: 25% fertile 75% el. accept and use[13]	couples: 10% of all use[15]	wives: 32-38% el. accept[16] fertile wives: 49% accept 39% use (only 8% use regularly for 4 mos. or more)[17]	wives: over 50% of all have tried for 6-9 mos. or more[18]			couples: 17% fertile accept[19]	couples: 17% of all use[15]
		eligible couples: 19% accept[21]	couples: 15% use[22]		couples: 16% use[23]	From November 1957, the use rate reached a fairly constant 20% for couples[24]			

that of the entire control population. It does not show a reduction achieved through the use of foam tablets. The reduction could only be shown if one assumed that the pregnancy rates of acceptors and of the entire control population were the same when the study began. The directors actually told the Advisory Committee that the effectiveness of the tablet was underestimated "because acceptors have a higher fertility performance than non-acceptors by 1.2:1."[13] No evidence was offered to substantiate this claim, and, in retrospect, there is good reason to doubt it. In light of the fact that the study's *sole* achievement in the field of birth control—as the directors finally admitted in the Book—was to "induce ... couples previously practicing birth control to switch to modern methods,"[14] we can assume that even before the study began, the fertility performance of the acceptors was *lower* than that of the entire control population. All the test did was to confirm this fact; it did not prove the effectiveness of foam tablets.

The future of the Khanna Study hinged on the results of the Pilot Study. The report to the Advisory Committee of April 3, 1956, said that the Pilot Study had confirmed that "25 percent of all fertile wives" and "75 percent of all eligible wives (couples) accept and use contraception." Yet, two and a half years later, the Pilot Study report maintained that the use rate for wives had been 13 percent, and the acceptance rate 19 percent. In fact, as the Pilot Study report stated, throughout its one year there were never more than 17 percent of the wives who used contraception.

It will be seen that on April 3, 1956, the Advisory Committee was told that the wives "accept and use" contraception. It is interesting that this is the first time some distinction is acknowledged between acceptance and use,

Table B
Pregnancy Rates[15]

(Pregnancy rate is defined as number of pregnancies occurring to married women, ages fifteen to forty-four, in 100 years of exposure to pregnancy)

	Months of exposure	No. of observed pregnancies	Pregnancy rate	Pregnancy rate as percentage of control village
Exploratory village				
September 1, 1954, to March 15, 1956				
Acceptors	446	11	29.6	43.5
Nonacceptors	269	20	89.3	
April 1, 1955, to March 15, 1956				
Acceptors using tablets only	191	5	31.5	46.5
Pilot experimental village				
April 1, 1955, to March 15, 1956				
Acceptors	322	12	44.7	67.5
Nonacceptors	568	32	67.6	
Control village				
April 1, 1955, to January 1, 1956				
All women ages 15-44	670	37	66.2	

even though the *assumption* is that those who accept also use. The study directors maintained to the Advisory Committee that it was only in December 1957, a year and a half after the Definitive Study had been financed and begun, that they realized there were several villagers who accepted contraceptives but did not use them. The impression of the staff was quite the opposite.

One of the two assistant field directors, Dr. Sohan Singh, maintained in an interview that "this distinction was realized in the Pilot Study itself." He also added that the staff "used to talk about this every day, but Dr. Wyon wrote the report."[16] As Dr. Singh explained, the field staff noticed a remarkable difference between the initial rates of acceptance of wives as against husbands in both the Exploratory and the Pilot villages. Female field workers had spent considerable time in the Exploratory village—where female acceptance was the highest—and their male counterparts had spent comparable time in the Pilot village—where male acceptance was the highest—before contraceptives were offered to people in either village. The conclusion was that the greater initial "acceptance" by women in one and men in the other village was the result of a desire to please rather than to use. Pandit Lahori Ram, one of the two workers in the Pilot Study, said that he realized that "some people were accepting the tablets but not using them" and had so reported as early as June 1955.[17]

Why had the study directors not made this clear to the Advisory Committee until long after the Definitive Study had been financed? In a rather candid response, the field director told me: "The great pressure on us from the Rockefeller Foundation and the Indian government was to promote acceptance of family planning. . . . We wanted very much to be successful. When we had high acceptance, why bother about use?"[18]

In its context, the remark was not a case of open cynicism, but one of rather honest retrospective self-analysis.

By the time the Definitive Study began, all major financial contributions to the Khanna Study had been made. Even so, the nature of the communications to the Advisory Committee did not change. As late as April 1957, the Progress Report to the Committee made no effort to even point out that accepting foam tablets was not necessarily equivalent to using them, but stated: "The results of the first year [of the Definitive Study] ... show a measure of acceptance that runs well above the level of 25 percent of eligible married women, as established by the experimental design, varying from 32 to 38 percent in different villages."[19]

The experimental design for the Definitive Study, as has been noted, was established on the basis of the results of the Pilot Study. It will be remembered that the experimental design did not establish a level of 25 *percent of eligible married women accepting* contraception, but a level of 75 *percent of eligible married women "accepting and using"* contraception.[20]

It was not until March 21, 1959, two years after the fact, that the Advisory Committee was told that during the first year of the Definitive Study—from April 1956 to March 1957—there had been a distinction between the acceptance and the use rate, and that although 49 percent of fertile wives accepted, only 8 percent of them used consistently for four months or more.[21]

The final meeting of the Advisory Committee was held on April 1, 1960, the day the field operations of the Khanna Study ended. By then it was quite obvious to the directors that the birth control program had been a failure. Yet there was not to be the slightest crack in the wall of optimism that they had so carefully constructed around their donors. The nature of the argument, to be sure, had changed. The Committee was told:

> During the four years of the main study, April 1956 to April 1960, use of foam tablets increased from 10 percent to 17 percent of all couples where the wife is of child-bearing age. This is an acceptance rate at least three times greater than that achieved in any similar study in India which has been published so far.[22]

And so, finally, the Khanna Study was held up as a *comparative* success!

Not only were the rates reported by the study directors to their financial donors *essentially* wrong, they were also *technically* incorrect. The controls that were built into the Khanna Study, and supervised by the Advisory Committee, were thus rendered totally ineffective. What was most important was that the information the Advisory Committee received came from the directors of the very study whose performance it was asked to judge. Inevitably, the Advisory Committee operated within the confines established by the directors of the study. The effect was to cloak reality and vitiate the apparatus of control.

The final set of communications prepared by the study directors—the Book—was meant for the interested public and came as a comprehensive account published after the completion of the Follow-up Study in 1969. The Book rewrites the story in such a way as to eliminate any impression of exaggerated optimism by the Khanna Study directors during the course of the study. The rates from March 1956 to March 1958 range from 15 percent to 24 percent (see Table A), while several definitions are used to justify these modest but remarkably consistent results.

The result is inevitably a number of serious inconsistencies among the various reports. For example, for March 1956, the date the Pilot Study was completed, the Pilot Study report states that 13 percent of the wives "used" contraception, the report to the Advisory Committee maintains that 75 percent of eligible wives "accepted and used" contraception, and the Book claims that 19 percent of eligible couples "accepted" contraception. Though published in 1971, the Book makes no mention of the "use" of contraception on that date, although the figures are available. When the discussion progresses to the Definitive Study, the reader of the Book is told that from November 1957, "the use rate reached a fairly constant 20 percent" for couples. For the same period, three reports had been circulated among the staff that gave the use rate as being 10 percent, 12 percent, and "about 15 percent"—but never 20 percent.

The field work of the Khanna Study lasted for a period of six years, from 1954 to 1960. The Book gives rates for only a period of two years, from 1956 to 1958. It leaves out the beginning two years, when the expectations were the most exaggerated, and the last two years, when the rates were at their lowest.

Notes

1. *Agenda* for the third meeting of the Advisory Committee (October 8, 1955), p. 1.
2. *Minutes* of the second meeting of the Advisory Committee (February 26, 1955), p. 2.
3. *Report* to the Advisory Committee (April 3, 1956), p. 2.
4. *Progress Report, 1955*, p. 11.

5. Ibid.

6. *Report* to the Advisory Committee, Table 4.

7. *Exploratory Investigations I*, p. 279.

8. Interview with Dr. John B. Wyon (November 12, 1970).

9. Ibid.

10. *Report* to the Advisory Committee, p. 2.

11. *Pilot Study*, p. S. 1.

12. *Report* to the Advisory Committee, p. 2.

13. Ibid., p. 3.

14. *The Khanna Study*, p. 298.

15. Table B is reproduced from Table 2 in the *Report* to the Advisory Committee.

16. Interview with Dr. Sohan Singh (July 8, 1970).

17. Interview with Pandit Lahori Ram (August 6, 1970).

18. Interview with Dr. John B. Wyon (November 12, 1970).

19. *Progress Report, April 1957*, p. 2.

20. *Report* to the Advisory Committee, p. 2.

21. *Agenda* for the sixth Advisory Committee meeting (March 21, 1959), p. 5.

22. *Minutes* of the Advisory Committee meeting (April 1, 1960), p. 2.

Notes to Table A

1. *Exploratory Investigations I*, p. 277.

2. Ibid, p. 279.

3. John E. Gordon, *Exploratory Investigations II*, Population Dynamics, Chakohi Village, Punjab, India, April 1, 1955, to March 31, 1956, p. 132 (study report issued in November 1957).

4. *Pilot Study*, p. S. 20.

5. *Use of contraception during the first year of offer in seven Punjab villages up to March 1958*, p. 1 (staff report).

6. Ibid., p. 3.

7. Ibid., p. 6.

8. *Use of contraception in seven Punjab villages, April 1955 to March 1958* (staff report), p. 3.

9. *Progress Report, 1955*, p. 11.

10. *Report* to the Advisory Committee (April 3, 1956), p. 2.

11. *Minutes* of the second meeting of the Advisory Committee (February 26, 1955), p. 1.
12. *Progress Report, 1955*, p. 12.
13. *Agenda* for the third meeting of the Advisory Committee (October 8, 1955), p. 1.
14. *Report* to the Advisory Committee, p. 2.
15. *Minutes* of the Advisory Committee meeting (April 1, 1960), p. 2.
16. *Progress Report, April 1957*, p. 2.
17. *Agenda* for the sixth Advisory Committee meeting (March 21, 1959), p. 5.
18. *Minutes* of the Advisory Committee meeting (October 29, 1957), p. 3.
19. *Extract* from the minutes of the meeting of the Advisory Committee (March 21, 1959), p. 1.
20. *The Khanna Study*, p. 42.
21. Ibid., p. 141.
22. Ibid.
23. Ibid., p. 47.
24. Ibid., p. 141.

Bibliography

Khanna Study Material

UNPUBLISHED MATERIAL

1. *Reports to the Advisory Committee*
Original Plan of Analysis, July 1953
      Part 1: Public Health Aspects
      Part 2: The Epidemiologic Approach
      Part 3: Plan of the Study
      Part 4: Statement of the Project
      Part 5: Progress Report, 1955
      Part 6: Extracts from Dr. Gordon's Diary
Progress Report up to 1954. For use of Advisory Board only (Unsigned).
John E. Gordon. *First Annual Report,* December 31, 1954.
Progress Report, 1955 (Unsigned).
John E. Gordon. *Progress Report, April 1957.*

2. *Advisory Committee meetings: minutes, reports, and agendas.*

Minutes of the second meeting of the Advisory Committee of the India-Harvard-Ludhiana Population Study, held in the Committee Room of the Indian Red Cross Society, Red Cross Road, New Delhi, on February 26, 1955, from 10:00 A.M. to 1:15 P.M., signed, John B. Wyon, Secretary-Convener, Advisory Committee.

Agenda for the third meeting of the Advisory Committee of the India-Harvard-Ludhiana Population Study, to be held at New Delhi on October 8, 1955, signed, Dr. Carl E. Taylor.

Minutes of the third meeting of the Advisory Committee of the India-Harvard-Ludhiana Population Study, held in the Committee Room of the Tuberculosis Association of India, New Delhi, on October 8, 1955 from 10:30 A.M. to 1:30 P.M., signed, John B. Wyon, Secretary and Convener.

Report to the Advisory Committee, Khanna, April 3, 1956.

Agenda for the meeting of the Advisory Committee of the India-Harvard-Ludhiana Population Study, at Khanna at 9:30 A.M. on Wednesday, April 4, 1956.

Minutes of the Advisory Committee meeting of the India-Harvard-Ludhiana Population Study, held in the Indian Red Cross Society Building, New Delhi, at 10:00 A.M. on Thursday, October 29, 1957.

Agenda for the sixth meeting of the Advisory Committee of the India-Harvard-Ludhiana Population Study, to be held on Saturday, March 21, 1959, at 10:00 A.M. in the Music Room, Hotel Cecil, Delhi.

Extract from the minutes of the meeting of the Advisory Committee of the India-Harvard-Ludhiana Population Study, held on Saturday, March 21, 1959, at 10:00 A.M. in the Music Room of Hotel Cecil, Delhi, signed John B. Wyon, Secretary, April 10, 1959, Khanna.

Minutes of the meeting of the Advisory Committee of the India-Harvard-Ludhiana Population Study, held in Claridge's Hotel, New Delhi, April 1, 1960 (first draft).

Interim Report of the India-Harvard-Ludhiana Population Study, covering the period April 1953 to April 1969, prepared for the Government of India, Health Ministry.

3. *Staff reports*

John E. Gordon and John B. Wyon. *A field study of motivation to family planning.* (No date.)

John B. Wyon, *Design of a special study to determine factors which influence the decision of village people to use or not to use contraceptives.* July 4, 1957.

John B. Wyon, *Need for an effort to increase the strength of desire of Punjab people to achieve small families.* April 11, 1958.

Use of contraceptives in seven Punjab villages, April 1955 to March 1958. (Issued by the India-Harvard-Ludhiana Population Study on May 6, 1958.)

Use of contraception during the first year of offer in seven Punjab villages up to March 1958. (Issued by the India-Harvard-Ludhiana Population Study on July 16, 1958.)

Proposed field work for anthropologist in Chakohi: July to September 1959. (Unsigned, dated July 19, 1959.)

4. *Study reports*

John E. Gordon. *Exploratory Investigations I*, Population Dynamics, Chakohi Village, Punjab, India, June 1954 to March 1955. (Issued in October 1956.)

John E. Gordon. *Exploratory Investigations II*, Population Dynamics, Chakohi Village, Punjab, India, April 1, 1955, to March 31, 1956. (Issued in November 1957.)

Pilot Study, 1st April 1955 to 31st March 1956. India-Harvard-Ludhiana Population Study, Report IV. (Issued in November 1958.)

PUBLISHED REPORTS

Wyon, John B., and John E. Gordon. *The Khanna Study: Population Problems in the Rural Punjab.* Cambridge, Mass.: Harvard University Press, 1971.

Interviews

Dr. John E. Gordon, Study Director, Cambridge, Mass., October 26, 1970.

Dr. John B. Wyon, Field Director, Boston, Mass., April 28, 1970; May 6, 1970; May 18, 1970; May 22, 1970; November 12, 1970.

Dr. Sohan Singh, Assistant Field Director, Chandigarh, Punjab, July 8, 1970.

Dr. Helen Gideon, Assistant Field Director, New Delhi, India, June 22, 1970.

Mr. Prakash Chandra Sekhri, New Delhi, India, June 24, 1970.

Mrs. Prakash Chandra Sekhri, New Delhi, India, June 24, 1970.

Mr. A. K. Padmanabha, Medak, Andhra Pradesh, June 16, 1970.

Pandit Lahori Ram, Jallunder City, Punjab, August 6, 1970.

Mrs. Sampuran Singh Ghuman, Ranjeet Bagh, Punjab, August 14, 1970.

Mr. Sampuran Singh Ghuman, Ranjeet Bagh, Punjab, August 15, 1970.

Mr. Banta Singh Rai, Amritsar, Punjab, August 7, 1970.

Mrs. Banta Singh Rai, Amritsar, Punjab, August 7, 1970.

Mrs. Kulwant Rana, Khanna, Punjab, July 8, 1970.

Dr. Prem Vir Ghulati, New Delhi, India, August 14, 1970.

Other References

Agarwala, S. N. *A Demographic Study of Six Urbanising Villages*. Bombay: Asia Publishing House, 1970.

Banks, J. A. "Historical Sociology and the Study of Populations." *Daedalus*, Spring 1968.

Bettelheim, Charles. *India Independent*. New York: Monthly Review Press, 1968.

Berelson, Bernard. "KAP Studies on Fertility." In *Family Plan-*

ning and Population Programs: A Review of World Developments. Edited by Bernard Berelson. Chicago and London: University of Chicago Press, 1966.

Bhatia, Dipak. "India: A Gigantic Task." In *Family Planning Programs: An International Survey.* Edited by Bernard Berelson. New York: Basic Books, Inc., 1969.

Calvert, H. *The Wealth and Welfare of the Punjab: Being Some Studies in Punjab Rural Economics.* Lahore, 1922.

Chandrasekhar, S. "Cultural Barriers to Family Planning in Under-developed Countries." *Population Review: A Journal of Asian Demography,* vol. 1, no. 2, July 1957.

Chhabra, G. S. *Social and Economic History of the Punjab (1849-1901).* Jallunder City: S. Nagin & Co., 1962.

Chow, Lien-Ping. "Evaluation of the Family Planning Program in Taiwan, Republic of China." *The Journal of the Formosan Medical Association,* vol. 67, no. 7, July 28, 1968.

Dandekar, Kumudini. *Communication in Family Planning: Report on an Experiment.* Gokhale Institute of Politics and Economics, Poona 4. Asia Publishing House, 1967.

Dutte, Romesh. *The Economic History of India in the Victorian Age, 1837-1900,* vol. 2. First published in 1903; second publication by the Ministry of Information and Broadcasting, Government of India, 1960.

Easterlin, Richard A. "Effects of Population Growth on the Economic Development of Developing Countries." *The Annals of the American Academy of Political and Social Sciences,* vol. 369, January 1967.

Ehrlich, Paul. *The Population Bomb.* New York: Ballantine Books, Inc., 1968.

Freedman, Ronald. "The Sociology of Human Fertility: A Trend Report and Bibliography." *Current Sociology,* vol. 10-11, no. 2, 1961-62.

Freedman, Ronald et al. *Family Planning in Taiwan: An Experiment in Social Change.* Princeton: Princeton University Press, 1969.

Hauser, Philip M. "Family Planning and Population Programs: A Book Review Article." *Demography*, vol. 4, no. 1, 1967.

Kirk, Dudley. "Prospects for Reducing Natality in the Under-developed World." *The Annals of the American Academy of Political and Social Sciences*, vol. 369, January 1967.

Lewis, Oscar. *Village Life in Northern India*. Urbana: University of Illinois Press, 1958.

Lukács, Georg. *History and Class Consciousness: Studies in Marxist Dialectics*. Translated by Rodney Livingstone. Cambridge, Mass.: The M.I.T. Press, 1971.

Myrdal, Gunnar. *Asian Drama: An Inquiry into the Poverty of Nations*, vol. 2. New York: Random House, 1968.

The Population Council. "India: The Singur Study." In *Studies in Family Planning*, July 1963.

Ranadive, K. T.; Shanbag, K. G.; Gujarathi, K. J. "A Socio-Economic Survey of a Population Group in Relation to Family Planning." *Population Review*, vol. 5, no. 1, January 1961.

Schultz, Paul T. "Effectiveness of Family Planning in Taiwan: A Methodology for Program Evaluation." A Rand Corporation Paper, November 1969. Mimeographed.

Schultz, Paul T. "An Economic Model of Family Planning and Some Empirical Evidence from Puerto Rico." A Rand Corporation Paper. Mimeographed.

Sovani, N. V. and Kumudini Dandekar. *Fertility Survey of Nasik, Kolaba and Satara (North) Districts*. Gokhale Institute of Politics and Economics, Publication no. 31, Poona 4, 1955.

Srinivas, M. N. *Caste in Modern India*. Bombay: Asia Publishing House, 1962.

Trevaskis, H. K. *The Land of the Five Rivers: An Economic History of the Punjab from the Earliest Times to the Year of the Grace 1890*. Oxford: Oxford University Press, 1928.

Wu, Hsin-Ying. "A Demographic Study on the Relationships of Nuptiality, Child Mortality, and Attitude Toward Fertility to Actual Fertility in Hsue-Chia Township in Taiwan."

The Journal of the Formosan Medical Association, vol. 69, no. 5, May 28, 1970.

Yang, Jae Mo. "Fertility and Family Planning in South Korea." *Proceedings of the World Population Conference.* Belgrade, August 30-September 10, 1965.